INDIE AUTHOR CONFIDENTIAL 7
SECRETS NO ONE WILL TELL YOU ABOUT WRITING

M.L. RONN

Published by Author Level Up LLC.

Version 3.0

Cover Design by Pixelstudio.

Cover Art by jasoshulwathon.

Editing by BZ Hercules.

Time Period Covered in This Book: Q4 2021

Special thank you to the following people on Patreon who supported this book: Zhade Barnet, Stephen Frans, Michael Guishard, Jon Howard, Beth Jackson, Mojo Jojo, Megan Mong, Lynda Washington, and Etta Welk.

Some links in this book contain affiliate links. If you purchase books and services through these links, I receive a small commission at no cost to you. You are under no obligation to use these links, but thank you if you do!

For more helpful writing tips and advice, subscribe to the Author Level Up YouTube channel: www.youtube.com/authorlevelup.

ABOUT THIS SERIES

This isn't your typical writing self-help book. This series is a compilation of lessons learned from an indie author trying to walk the path to success. Follow author M.L. Ronn (Michael La Ronn) as he navigates what it means to master the craft of writing, marketing, and running a profitable publishing business. Learn from his successes and failures, and learn about things that most successful authors only talk about behind the scenes.

To read all the collected volumes of this series in an anthology, visit www.authorlevelup.com/confidential.

CONTENTS

BECOME A WORLD-CLASS CONTENT CREATOR

BECOME A WORLD-CLASS MARKETER

BECOME A TECHNOLOGY AND DATA-DRIVEN WRITER

BECOME THE WRITER OF THE FUTURE

INTRODUCTION

As 2021 comes to an end, I realize that this year was finally a "normal" year—as normal as things can get right now given the COVID-19 pandemic. This year flew by compared to 2020, which was like a decade packed into a year.

I started 2021 off strong but then faltered a little in Q2 as I changed jobs and finished my final semester of law school. I made up for lost time in Q4, which was my most productive quarter ever.

As I write this chapter, I'm nearing the end of my "Beast Mode" challenge, and I wrote 10 books between July 1st and October 15.

Now that I've finished law school, wrapped up podcasting, and am no longer teaching insurance classes, I have a lot more time on my hands, and it's showing up in my productivity. I have more focus than I ever had at the beginning of the year, and that feels great!

This volume concludes a great year for me, and a year where I got a lot done to put myself on solid footing in the future.

My Core Strategic Priorities

As a refresher, my mission is to create content that entertains and/or educates my audience, preferably both, and to remain nimble in an ever-changing industry. I do this by focusing on five strategic priorities:

- Become a world-class content creator
- Become a world-class marketer
- Become a technology-driven writer
- Become a data-driven writer
- Become the writer of the future

I believe these five priorities are most important for me to have a long-term, sustainable career.

Stay tuned for significant changes to my strategic priorities for 2022.

What's in This Volume

In the World-Class Content Creator section, I discuss the lessons that "Beast Mode" taught me this year as well as some major editing victories that drastically reduced the number of errors in my books.

In the World-Class Marketer section, I discuss lessons learned in public speaking engagements as well as some other miscellaneous topics. Also, due to updating my strategic priorities, this will be the last volume where I discuss marketing ideas.

In the Technology and Data-Driven section, I discuss some issues I had with data this year as well as experimenting with emerging tech. I also finally resolved to learn cover design.

In the Writer of the Future section, I discuss problems with being prolific, clothing that can potentially help you become a better writer, and major lessons learned in 2021.

Moving forward, I've decided to keep the series quarterly for now. I'll also be making some updates to the format of the book, which I'll discuss in the final chapter. These changes will streamline my process of creating the *Indie Author Confidential* series while improving the quality.

Enjoy this volume.

M.L. Ronn
October 15, 2021
Des Moines, Iowa

BECOME A WORLD-CLASS CONTENT CREATOR

LESSONS FROM RAT CITY

This quarter, I embarked on what was my most difficult writing task this year—restarting a novel that I left off in the middle of.

That novel was *Rat City: The Chicago Rat Shifter* Book 2.

The worst part about this novel was that when I stopped writing it, I was in a murky spot, and wasn't sure what was going to come next. That made it much more difficult to restart because I had to first remember what I wrote and then try to figure out where to take the novel.

I don't like doing cold restarts, so here's what I did to prepare for writing the story again:

I reread the first few chapters and the latest chapter.

For the first few days, I wrote 500 words, followed by rereading a chapter. I rinsed and repeated until I reread everything, which made it easier to push the story forward.

That worked so well that I didn't even notice when I was having regular word-count days at first.

However, my first few weeks had low word-count days. Normally, I write around 2000-3000 words per day when I'm writing fiction; for the first few weeks after restarting, I was lucky if I wrote more than 1500 words per day. The novel was slower than I am used to.

But *Rat City* taught me some valuable lessons:

At 76,000 words, it's my longest novel ever. My second-longest novel, *Old Wicked,* is 67,000 words.

When you write a novel that is beyond your stamina level, it's an intense exercise, especially when you're writing every day. I experienced several days of sheer mental exhaustion. This happens when you write consistently over your daily average. For example, during the last two weeks alone, I was writing well over 4000 words per day.

This story was the ultimate test of writing into the dark. It's extraordinarily complicated, with many plot twists. I continue to be amazed at how my creative voice stitches stories together.

There were many times when I thought I was coming up on the end, but I was nowhere close in retrospect. My mind kept playing tricks on me.

I rediscovered the joy of writing with a quota. I haven't historically been a quota guy, but implementing a 2000-word per day quota in the last quarter of the novel helped me finish it. I may revise my thoughts on quotas moving forward.

This story is the darkest story I've ever written. Sure, it's tame compared to a lot of authors, but I go into very weird territory: intense rat scenes, necromancy, demon possessions, and so on. There are serious consequences at the end of the story and it's not a happy-go-lucky ending like I normally write. It's a depressing ending, actually. The funny thing is that I didn't realize how dark the story was until I was self-editing it.

Normally, writing into the dark (without an outline) has a predictable series of events: you start off knowing absolutely nothing about the story, and as you progress, you slowly see where your brain is steering you. At some point around the 80- to 90-percent mark, there's the "glimmer," which I call the moment in the novel-writing process when you know exactly how the story is going to end. Once you see the glimmer, finishing is just a foregone conclusion and you just have to go through the motions. *Rat City* had a glimmer, but it was a very faint one, and this novel kept me on the edge of my seat until the final scene. I had no idea what would happen, which is scary for a lot of people, especially when you're writing a 76,000-word novel.

My "current tolerance" level for writing novels without outlines is around 60K. Under that amount, I can usually remember most details and keep all the threads together easily. I discovered with this novel that once I write over 60K, this task gets twice as hard. To be honest, I struggled to keep everything straight. It was a learning experience that taught me how to manage bigger novels. I don't have any difficulty with keeping the plot together; it's the little details that get me. For example, I remembered that my hero needed to meet a friend for ice cream. I forgot that my hero told the friend to meet her at a park. I just had the hero show up at the ice cream parlor. Little stuff like that adds up in a big way throughout a long novel. My current workflows aren't designed for big novels, and I need to change that.

I owe much of my success for this novel to waking up early in the mornings. Whether I was inspired or not, I woke up and wrote, and there's something to be said about that, even when I was staring at a blinking cursor for longer than I wanted.

I had a bout of "writer's block" around the 75-percent mark and I dissolved it very quickly with a new technique. My heroine needed to solve a problem, but I didn't know how to get her past it. I walked away from the computer and mowed the lawn. I told myself that I would listen to something—anything—and whatever I listened to, I would make it contain the answer. I happened to resume an audiobook about death called *The Five*

Invitations by Frank Ostaseski. He wrote something in the book that triggered an idea. When I finished mowing the lawn, I returned to my chair and charged full-speed ahead.

I tested out at least ten experimental writing techniques in the novel. With one, I switched from the third-person POV to the first-person; with another, I "bookended" an entire scene within a conversation between the hero and his mom, where the middle scene is an encounter with a villain—it all happens at the exact same time; I also wrote a scene that the hero imagines but doesn't actually happen, but the reader doesn't realize it until the scene is over; I wrote several scenes between two villains who are brothers, and the POV switches between them so that the reader can't directly see what's happening, but instead experience it through the brother who is also experiencing it secondhand. This novel was a training ground for a lot of fun techniques. Whether they work or not is another matter entirely.

Anyway, there are many more lessons that *Rat City* taught me, but I'm grateful for the experience it gave me.

LESSONS FROM COLD HARD MAGIC
(OR, A LEVEL UP)

In the previous chapter, I discussed my experience with *Rat City* (*The Chicago Rat Shifter, Book* 2). Two days after finishing that novel, I started writing another: *Cold Hard Magic* (*The Good Necromancer, Book* 2).

Both novels have a lot in common:

- I started writing them in a blaze of glory, but then had to stop for some reason or another.
- I stopped writing both novels at exactly the 50 percent mark.
- Both use a lot of experimental story techniques that readers will love or hate.
- I had zero idea what I was supposed to write next.

In *Cold Hard Magic's* case, I stopped writing the novel in late 2019, just before the pandemic started.

This novel had many similarities and differences with *Rat City*.

The biggest similarity is that I started the novel cold. I just sat down and started writing. That's extremely difficult and taxing, and because you don't always remember what you wrote before and you don't always know what to write next!

However, I did it anyway because I knew the only way to finish was to start, no matter how painful. The difference with this novel was that I started with a quota. It took me several days to ramp up to "ground effect" with *Rat City*. It's amazing how, because I set a 2000-word quota for *Cold Hard Magic,* that I managed to exceed that quota every day for a week, which led me to finish the novel expeditiously. I had more zero word-count days than I would have liked with *Rat City*, but I didn't have any with *Cold Hard Magic,* though there were times when I had zero clue what to write.

That's the power of quotas.

Overall, though, *Cold Hard Magic* was an easier and shorter novel to write. It clocked in at about 50,000 words. It was easier to keep the different plot threads straight too.

This novel also reinforced a concept that I learned early on when I learned how to write into the dark: the best answer may be behind you.

Much like *Rat City*, this novel took a few left turns that I didn't see coming.

It was such a left turn that I second-guessed myself. Late last night, I was lying in bed thinking, "This is crazy. I don't know about this."

I kept thinking that maybe I overwrote part of the final battle—sometimes when you write into the dark, you go down avenues that you don't ultimately use, so you have to throw some words away. It's part of the process. I wondered if this had happened. I was in the middle of the final battle and hit a wall. I had no idea what was going to happen, and that's unusual this late in a novel.

So, I slept on it.

The next morning, I decided to review the entire novel. I

gave it a quick read to see if there was anything I forgot when I was writing the last quarter of the novel.

Sometimes, when you write into the dark and don't know what to do next, the answer is most often behind you.

It's like when you're on an airplane and the flight attendant says, "Please note that the nearest exit may be behind you." In a crisis, people don't always remember that.

Anyway, I reviewed the novel, particularly a few sections that I wasn't sure about. Sure enough, my creative voice remained true. It had planted ALL the seeds for the final battle. I was just too stubborn to realize it. In fact, some of the lines I write very early in the first couple of chapters were almost eerily prescient when you read what happens in the final battle. I had zero idea where this story was going, and it's still awe-inspiring to me how your mind will tell a story if you let it. Your first job is to simply get out of the way and give your mind what it needs. Your second job is to listen.

In my case, the answer was familiarizing myself with what I wrote.

I returned to the final chapter, and the next thing I knew, I was typing the final sentence.

So, remember, if you get stuck in a novel while writing into the dark, the answer is probably behind you. *Cold Hard Magic* helped me re-learn that important lesson.

ONE OF THE BEST PARTS ABOUT THIS JOB: THE FAN MAIL (OR, A PERMAFREE UPDATE)

Last quarter, when I published *Authors, Steal This Book: 67 Business Ideas for the Writer of the Future*, I had no idea what would happen. The book is now successfully permafree at most retailers and it is starting to accumulate anywhere from a dozen to two dozen downloads per day. I'm seeing a slight increase in sales of my other writing books, and that's a good thing.

However, the real test of success is whether my ideas have an impact.

I received an email from a *New York Times*-bestselling author who was in his mid-seventies and just starting on his self-publishing journey. (Yes, you read that right.) He was fed up with traditional publishing and wanted to reach readers directly. While this author isn't a household name, he wrote a book that many avid book readers in his genre would recognize. Random circumstances led him to my book and he downloaded it. When he read my chapter on "Pilot Series" (series where you have readers give you feedback on whether to write it or not), it inspired an idea that he felt so passionate about, he emailed me on the spot. He's going to be testing that idea with a new series he's writing.

How cool is that?

Sometimes I'm amazed at where my books travel. I'm honored when people reach out and let me know how my writing has impacted them. I hope that the pilot series idea works well for him.

Now, if one of my books could just land in the hands of a celebrity who wants to feature me on their platform...

WHAT MAGIC MUSHROOMS AND WRITING INTO THE DARK HAVE IN COMMON

I've been watching news stories discussing the use of psychedelic drugs. There have been studies that have shown that they are effective in treating PTSD and ameliorating terminal cancer patients' conditions, among other things.

I listened to several interviews with psychedelic experts who discussed the benefits of the drugs in certain situations.

(No, I'm not going to do magic mushrooms. However, what they said was intriguing. I won't pretend to be an expert on this topic, but I'll summarize some of the takeaways as I understood them.)

One of the effects of psychedelic drugs is what is called "ego death," which is defined as a detachment of the soul from the body. Some people report it feels as if you are actually dying, but it's ultimately a transcendence that helps people explore themselves and become more self-aware. Terminal cancer patients who undergo ego death can become more comfortable with dying for real. Ego death can help someone with PTSD move past trauma.

When one takes a psychedelic, it is recommended to do it under the watch of an experienced guide, someone who understands what the drug will do to you so they can help you through the process. You also want someone with you to "hold space"—someone who will not be taking the drug, but will be there to provide you emotional support. You also need a safe space.

The result of an effective psychedelic session is mind expansion and self-awareness, among other things.

What does this have to do with writing?

I've been getting many questions about writing into the dark lately, and I happened to receive a question about it on the same day I was listening to an interview about psilocybin (magic mushrooms). That got me thinking about how writing into the dark and consuming psychedelics have a lot in common:

- They're both illegal ("pantsing" is frowned upon in the writing world).
- They provide deep insights into yourself that is hard to put into words.
- They're best experienced under the tutelage of a guide and someone who can hold space for you.

Writing into the dark is exactly that: writing into the dark. You start a story with no idea how it will end, and you keep sitting down and working on it until you finish it. I can't overstate enough how extraordinarily difficult this is for writers to do. I glamorize it and make it look easier than it actually is. It requires self-confidence, courage, and faith in yourself.

I suspect that many authors fear writing into the dark because they don't have a structure. It feels scary to them. This was true for me until I read Dean Wesley Smith's book, which served as a guide for me.

In my monthly power-hour livestreams, I frequently field questions about writing into the dark. I often end up giving advice to writers about how to get through their manuscript because they're stuck and aren't sure how to proceed. I've become sensitive to the feelings that people experience throughout the process as well as my own feelings when I'm writing without an outline. Most of the questions I receive are about the emotional side of writing into the dark.

I've learned a lot, mainly that:

- Writing your first book into the dark is always the hardest; it gets much easier after the first time (but the first time is a bitch, let me tell you).
- Every book is a test. Every book will test you in different ways. If you finish the book, you pass, even if the story fails to resonate with readers.
- Every book requires a different approach when you're in the dark. Once you've done it for a while, you intuitively know what the book needs, but this knowledge comes with experience and it is difficult to explain to beginners.

I've decided to write a book about my process of writing into the dark. I will talk about the technical, emotional, and practical sides of it. I hope that the book will be a guide for writers and hold space for them as they go through the process.

It's amazing how unrelated ideas come together and result in a book idea.

TWO EDITING VICTORIES

I sent the manuscript for my novel *Cold Hard Magic* (*The Good Necromancer Book* 2) to my editor.

Cold Hard Magic is technically the first novel to benefit from the efficiencies of my new editing workflow. It took me two previous novels to tweak it.

My benchmarks for editing are approximately 275 edits per novel, which is around 1 edit per 200 words or so.

To my surprise, this novel came back with 179 edits! That's 34 percent lower than my average!

It wasn't an accident. It was a culmination of the process I created (and discussed in the previous volumes of this series). It's also a testament to the power of owning your data and using it to become a world-class content creator.

Cold Hard Magic is officially the cleanest novel I have ever sent to an editor. At 50,000 words, it's a standard-length book for me. To put it into perspective, my writing books are usually very clean when I send them to my editor. *Cold Hard Magic* was cleaner than some of those, which is a feat. Most people agree that it's harder to write clean fiction than nonfiction.

Then came the second victory.

My novel *Dead Rat Walking* (The Chicago Rat Shifter Book 1) is 60,000 words. It received 384 total edits. This is not an apples-to-apples comparison to *Cold Hard Magic*. This novel went through a copyedit and a proofread, whereas *Cold Hard Magic* only received a copyedit. This was also the first novel I used my editing workflow on. It is also a more complex novel, which is why my total edit count is higher than my average of around 275 edits.

Here's where things get interesting. *Rat City* (*The Chicago Rat Shifter* Book 2) is considerably longer at 76,000 words, but it received 370 total edits despite being 27 percent bigger!

That's amazing. It is evidence that my editing process is working.

I'm pretty proud of these accomplishments. Will my next novel demonstrate the same results? I don't know, but this appears to be a positive sign that my editing analytics approach is working, and it's making a real difference in how clean my manuscripts are.

All of this happened because I was lying in bed one night and had this idea that I couldn't let go. I kept exploring it because I didn't know how, but I felt in my gut that it would take me somewhere. Funny how that works.

The work isn't over. I need to keep using insights and following the data to find additional ways to cut down on repetitive edits. But this is definitely a moment for celebration!

WRITING AT GROUND EFFECT

I read a blog article by Kristine Kathryn Rusch, who talked about "ground effect" in writing. I recommend you read her blog article, but here is a summary of the idea:

- "Ground effect" is an aviation term for when a plane is landing, but it does not seem to want to land; instead, it feels as if it could keep traveling forever, using the ground as a cushion.
- In writing, Kris talks about how her husband Dean Wesley Smith and writer friend Matt Buchman adapted "ground effect" as a way to describe their writing productivity. When they wrote for several days in a row, they'd achieve "ground effect," and it would be much easier to write on subsequent days. However, whenever they missed a day, it was a lot harder to get back to ground effect.

In some respects, this reminds me of Newton's First Law: an object at rest will remain at rest and an object in motion will remain in motion until acted upon by a net external force. It's a lot of work to roll a boulder up a hill, but once you get going, it's easier. But heaven help you if that boulder comes to a full stop.

I've been thinking about this blog article and how it's also true for me. Historically, I've been so busy that I simply could not write every day. It was impossible when I was working a full-time job, raising a family, and attending law school classes in the evenings. Now that my calendar is emptier, I'm finding that it's easier to write every day. More interestingly, I'm finding that every day I write breeds another equal or better writing word count the next day.

When I wrote my novel *Rat City*, I hit ground effect very quickly at the beginning but lost it around the 25 percent mark and didn't recover until the 75 percent mark. Roughly half of the novel was me struggling to get back to ground effect. Some of the low word-count days were because of circumstances outside of my control, but I noticed that whenever I missed a day, I would miss for several more days until I could hit ground effect again.

There's something to be said about momentum. I've said for a while that good word-count days are almost always followed by bad word-count days. That's true for me.

This got me thinking about some observations on writing (at least for me):

During any given novel, the very high and very low word-count days almost cancel each other out. The real progress is in the days where you're writing closer to your average.

Good writing days breed more good writing days and writing days where you "miss" breed more misses.

Once you have written a certain number of words, you will hit ground effect, which makes it easy to write for a long period.

It's always interesting to read about how other writers think about their productivity.

HOW I'M TRYING TO READ MORE

In writing the chapter about ground effect and writing, I realized that this is true of other areas in my life.

For the last few years, I've struggled with balancing writing and reading. With my crazy schedule, I often had to choose whether I would write, market, or read for any given day. Since I'm trying to grow my writing business, I often chose to write.

My experience is that it's never a good idea to pit writing and reading against each other. If you're an ambitious author like me, reading will almost always lose. That's why I listen to audiobooks—they help me continue reading books quickly.

I still read more books than the average person, but I don't read anywhere near the level I used to, which was one or two full-sized books per week. I desperately want to get back to that, but I know that it won't be possible as long as I work a full-time job.

Anyway, I noticed that when I have long streaks of reading every day, reading is easier. When I've been away from a book for a while, I struggle to get back into it. This is a basic observation, but something I've been aware of lately as I reconfigure my life to a new "normal" after scaling back many of my activities.

CREATING A HARDCOVER BOOK
FOR THE FIRST TIME

Earlier this year, Amazon KDP introduced the worst-kept private beta of all time: hardcovers. I've had access to it for a while but didn't say anything because of a non-disclosure agreement (which was the worst-kept non-disclosure of all time). However, now the NDA is lifted, and just about everybody knows about the program...

I still think it's a better idea to go with Ingram Spark for hardcovers, but I do like that Amazon provides the option now. I don't want to be tied to Amazon's ecosystem, so I decided to break down and buy ISBNs (more on that later).

I decided to test out hardcover editions with my *Chicago Rat Shifter* series. The first book is 60K and the second book is 76K, so they're great candidates for a hardcover edition.

I simply emailed my designer and asked them to design a new hardcover print edition. It cost $50.

I signed up with Ingram Spark, who offers a special deal for members of The Alliance of Independent Authors (ALLi). Normally, they charge you to set up a book in their system, and they also charge for every revision. ALLi members get those fees waived. (Have you joined ALLi yet?)

I ordered proof versions of the hardcovers just to test them out and see the quality.

Not bad. I'm happy with how they turned out.

Finally, I published them. It's pretty cool to have hardcover editions for sale. They look great on a bookshelf. I should have done this a long time ago, but hey, it's never too late to do anything in self-publishing.

Moving forward, I'll create hardcovers for my books when it makes sense. I'll probably do it for all books over 50K—I don't think smaller books look good in hardcover, but that's a personal opinion.

A NEW APPROACH TO OUTLINING (IN THE DARK)

In a previous chapter, I discussed lessons I learned while writing my novel *Rat City*. It is the longest novel I have written to date, and it taught me some valuable lessons.

One of those lessons is that my current outlining process doesn't work for longer novels.

I write my novels "into the dark," which means that I write them without an outline. However, as I finish chapters, I document what I wrote. This is the outline I'm referring to. A plotter used an outline to help them figure out what to write; a writer who writes into the dark uses an outline to capture what they wrote. This, outlining when you're writing into the dark, is a practical tool, and your outlines are always 100 percent accurate (compared to plotter's outlines, which may not be).

Before *Rat City*, my outlining processes were as follows:

- I wrote a chapter.
- I created an outline that listed the POV, characters present, location, summary, and any character details.
- Rinse and repeat.

However, with *Rat City*, that process didn't work. I started noticing problems.

The first was that my outline, while accurate at the macro level, wasn't helping me keep track of *micro* details in the story. For example, there is a character who has chains running down his torso and legs in Chapter 20. Those chains become very important near the end of the story...but I accidentally described them as ropes instead! Naturally, I caught the problem and corrected it, but my outline should have helped me avoid that. It didn't.

The second problem was my characters' actions. In one chapter, I had my hero agree to meet a friend for ice cream. When I first wrote the draft, he tells her to meet him at a park entrance and they'll walk over to the parlor. But when it's time to meet, I had him show up at the parlor instead, where she was waiting for him. In another scene, my heroine agrees to meet his mom for a birthday gathering, but her mom shows up at her house!

In other words, the characters' actions didn't reflect their words. There were lots of little problems like this that I easily fixed during self-editing, but there were more of these issues than I like to see. Usually, my drafts are clean. *Rat City* was not.

There are also other elements that need to be closely tracked during drafting, such as any injuries characters sustain, wardrobe changes, and so on.

I thought about my outlining process. Is there a way I can manage details more precisely so that I don't create these sorts of issues moving forward? Nothing makes a reader put a book down faster than continuity errors.

Is there a way I can use my outline better so that I can write the story consistently? I am fine with spending a little more time on the outline if needed.

I recently switched to Microsoft Excel for my outlines. I like

Excel better because I house my Editing Analytics Chapter Scoring Model there (see previous volumes for more information). I thought, "Since I'm using Excel for outlining, what if I used it to improve my outlining process?"

Most importantly, I wanted to find answers to the following questions:

- How can I outline so effectively that I don't need to read the novel again?
- How can I use an outline to help me keep the *series* consistent?

My initial idea was to create a form macro that would capture the important details and store them in a database that I could refer to throughout the novel (or series). The database would help me manage my story more globally. However, that was too complicated and would have required time and money, which I didn't want to spend.

I ended up amending my outline so that I captured more of the micro details.

Here was the result.

I tested the method by redoing the outline for *Dead Rat Walking* and capturing micro details. Not surprisingly, I found some very minor issues that needed correcting. Nothing serious —just little details that most people won't notice.

The outline also lets me see the story not as a story, but as a series of data points. For example, I can filter the outline down to all the chapters with a certain character and then track their appearance over time.

For example, the hero's sister in *Dead Rat Walking* has a distinct look: blonde ponytail, starry-night bandanna, stud in her cheek, dragoon tattoo on her arm, and a camo tank top.

When I filtered down to her chapters, I noticed that I

described her well in the first couple of chapters, but then I failed to describe her in the middle of the book. Using the Excel sheet, I quickly found the chapters where she needed a little characterization, and I used this knowledge to surgically add some details that were consistent with the description above, like the hero seeing her ponytail bob across the bar, or her untying her bandanna and tying it again in a messy knot over her head. Or coffee stains on her camo tank top because she owns a coffee shop. Just a little characterization is all the reader needs. My new outline method helped me identify surgical gaps like this one.

There's no doubt in my mind that this outlining method is much better. It's effective for small *and* large novels. It takes me a little more time with the outline. Before the new method, it took me approximately two minutes to jot down the events and details of each chapter. This new process will take me approximately seven minutes per chapter. That's around 3.5 hours outlining for a 40-chapter novel.

But consider the benefits:

- By forcing myself to *write down* the micro details in summary form, I'm more likely to remember them later.
- The micro details are well-organized, succinctly written, and easy to sort and filter on the spreadsheet.

This minor enhancement to my workflow should help me write cleaner first drafts faster and more effectively.

ANOTHER OUTLINING TEST

My new outlining method worked so well for my *The Chicago Rat Shifter* series that I wanted to apply it to my current *The Good Necromancer* series.

The two series couldn't be more different. *The Good Necromancer* is written in the first-person POV and the books are shorter and easier to manage. *The Chicago Rat Shifter* series is written in the third-person POV and the books are much bigger and have more details.

More importantly, the flow of information in the novels is different. When you're writing in the third-person POV, you divulge details about characters and settings in a traditional, matter-of-fact way. They're presented as facts. In the first-person, information is presented as an opinion—the character will say something and then make an opinion about another character. The result is that first-person novels tend to be richer with world-building information, at least in my experience.

This is a problem when you're building an outline for writing into the dark.

Let me give you an example. In *The Good Necromancer* series, Lester's friend CeCe is a lich, which is a supernatural warden of the dead. He says in the novel, "In supernatural terms, CeCe is what we call a lich. A lich is an immortal warden of the dead, and a necromancer of the highest degree. They control the dead and prepare them to either ascend to the next plane or shatter from existence. Everything that happens in the spirit realm happens under the watch of the liches. They're smart, organized, and vengeful—not supernatural beings you want to cross. If you steal from them, they'll steal from you, only two times as bad. And if you delay their retribution by running away, they'll place a doom and a curse on your soul, wait patiently for you to die, and harvest you into the worst kind of undead servitude.

"When a necromancer of extraordinary ability dies, they can become a lich if they so choose, but only with the permission of the Lich King, who is tough to please. Trust me, I would know."

How does one classify the information that Lester shares? These aren't character details per se, and they're not setting details. It's simply lore of the world, which is very hard to capture systematically.

I found that my new outlining method didn't work as well with *The Good Necromancer*. The original outlines are pretty good. That said, I can see forgetting details in this series just like I did with *The Chicago Rat Shifter* series.

Here's how I decided to address the issue:

- Use the new outlining method for the series, including *Cold Hard Magic* (*Book* 2) because it's still useful.
- When I pick up Book 2, I'll read the outline first, followed by the first three chapters, ending with the last three chapters that lead to the current point where I left off. Then I'll start writing.

- When I start writing, I'll do a master loop. For example, if I pick up on Chapter 18, once I finish the chapter, I'll loop Chapter 18 and then review Chapter 1. Once I finish Chapter 19, I'll loop that chapter and then review Chapter 2. And so on.
- Every time I finish a chapter, I will review the same chapter in the previous books. For example, once I finish Chapter 18, I'll review Chapter 18 in Book 1 and Book 1.5. This will help me connect more dots as I stitch the series together.

We will see how this goes. The more books you have in a series, the more work you have to do to keep everything consistent.

A THIRD OUTLINING TEST

This summer, I wrote a book about writing apps. I designed the book to be an edition-type book, meaning that it would be one that I revisit every few years because some of the information might be outdated.

Normally, I try not to write books that have a shelf life. It's not a smart long-term strategy to have to keep updating your books' content. However, I felt I had no other choice with this book, and the content demanded it.

When I write fiction, I outline my novels as I go. The outline becomes a reference document that helps me remember what happened.

Occasionally, I'll outline nonfiction. Mostly, I create a short table of contents of the different benefits I want people to get from the book, but it's not anything elaborate.

With my writing app book, I had to *plan* for obsolescence. I had to predict, as much as possible, which sections would most likely need to be updated in the future, and then I had to capture that information so I could access it. My goal is to make any needed edits as quickly as possible. How do I accomplish that?

I created an outline in Microsoft Excel. My worksheet had two tabs. The first tab tracked snippets of content that might need to be updated.

The second tab tracked all images in the book. This book has a *lot* of images (also another thing that is against common wisdom). I numbered each image on the spreadsheet, which corresponds to the image's file name. This way, I can identify which images need to be swapped quickly.

Thus concludes how I "outlined" a writing book for the first time. Will it work? No idea, but we'll see. It's better than doing nothing!

SOME QUICK MATH TO SUPPORT
DAILY WRITING QUOTAS

I've often discussed how I have not been a writer who writes every day. I discussed this a little in a previous chapter.

Now that I have more time in my day, I've come around to the power of word quotas.

James Scott Bell said something that has always stuck with me over the years: to paraphrase, he said the only reason he is a career writer is because he adheres to a strict quota every day, rain or shine. I love that sentiment and want to do the same thing.

The question I asked: what should my quota be? I don't want a number that's too low, but I also don't want one that is too high.

I settled on 2000 words no matter whether it's fiction or nonfiction. My quota is in effect for six days a week, with a slightly easier 1000-word quota on Sundays.

Two thousand words a day of nonfiction is doable for me and 2000 of fiction is a slight stretch, particularly when I'm starting a new book or in a rough spot. How would my habits change with a quota? How would that affect writer's block?

At the time of this writing, I've been on a three-week streak and I've exceeded the quota every day.

A quota gives me great flexibility: on days where I hit the quota early, I don't have to continue writing—I can market, read, or do something else related to the writing business and know that I'm on a good path. Or, I can keep writing as if I have no quota. Either way, I benefit from having a day where the foundation is built on a solid word count.

Two thousand words per day is:

- One 50,000-word novel approximately 25 days
- 12.48 novels per year (assuming one month off)

That's only if you meet the quota! Imagine what these numbers would be with a consistent, healthy number of higher word days. It wouldn't be hard to exceed one million words per year, which is out of this world.

Those numbers add up fast. They have inspired me to keep a quota. This is a break from how I've conducted my writing business in the past, so we'll see how it goes.

QUALITY ASSURANCE CHECKLIST

At almost every job in the world, there is someone who checks your work. Quality Assurance (QA) is one of the most anxiety-inducing and infuriating terms you can ever utter to someone on the job.

Some workplaces dangle QA scores over employees' heads like carrots, making them chase the impossibility of perfection. In other jobs, QA exists to sabotage and destroy people's prospects of success.

Everybody wants to get better at their jobs, everybody makes mistakes, everybody accepts that they're human, and (almost) everybody will graciously forgive the mistakes of others, but *nobody* likes being called out for their own mistakes. In some ways, QA is as human as humanity itself—full of contradictions.

What does QA look like for an author? For starters, there's no one breathing down your back, waiting for you to screw up. In my estimation, we already come out ahead based on that fact alone.

We can use QA truly as a way to get better, because we know that releasing better books will lead to better sales.

Here's how I'm thinking about QA across my writer plat-form. I want to eliminate:

- typos and spelling errors in my books, book descriptions, and website
- inconsistent story details
- broken links in my books and on my site
- anything that creates a poor reader experience

What if I put together a checklist of items to check for? Each item would be a pass or fail. I could give that checklist to an assistant who could do the checking for me so that I have a neutral third party reviewing my platform. It would cost a little money, but any mistakes they find are probably costing me money anyway. This would be akin to an "audit" at a workplace. (I know, I shuddered when I wrote that last sentence, but you can't deny that this is a legitimate problem that an "audit" can fix!)

I could hire an assistant to do a platform audit every year or biannually. It's a great idea and a smart use of money.

ESTIMATING E-BOOK DELIVERY FEES

With my book *The Writing App Handbook,* I put a lot of images in it.

Images are a big no-no in e-books. The common wisdom is to not include images or think twice about the ones you do. I usually agree with this wisdom.

However, this book needed images. You can't write a book on writing apps and not show people how they work! Honestly, a book is not the most elegant format to showcase this information, but I had an idea and I wanted to see what would happen if I executed it.

The Writing App Handbook has 73 images. All of them are screenshots from different writing apps on different operating systems.

The book is organized by features. Each chapter explains what the feature is generally and how it often shows up on different apps. I then illustrate this point by using screenshots of the feature in action.

It's a unique concept that I haven't seen in the writing space. I have no idea if it will work or not.

Anyway, with that many images, I have to worry about e-book delivery fees on Amazon. They charge $0.10 per megabyte, and the fee is subtracted from the commission of the book.

First, I made sure I compressed my images using free online websites. That reduced my average file size per image by about 50 percent.

Second, I estimated the delivery fee to help me pick the best price for the book. Did I need to charge more for this book to offset the delivery fees?

I used a quick Excel spreadsheet to make a rough estimate of what the delivery fee would be for each price point.

I estimated that my file size would be around 4 MB, and it ended up being 3.3 MB, which is actually pretty good, all things considered. At $4.99, I'm still clearing $3.00. With a more modest delivery, I would usually clear $3.30.

So, I decided that $4.99 was an appropriate price point. I was willing to sacrifice the additional $0.30.

We'll see how this book does, but this was an exercise I've never had to do before. My first novel had over 100 images, but I wasn't wise enough to think about compression, delivery fees, and price points before I published it.

LESSONS FROM MICHAEL CRICHTON

This year, I've been studying the works of Michael Crichton. I considered him a "virtual mentor," one whose work I learn from at my own pace, even though I don't know him and will never be able to meet him because he passed away in 2008.

Michael Crichton is the author of hit novels, such as *Jurassic Park*, *The Andromeda Strain*, and *Timeline*. He was also a producer and director of movies like *Westworld* and TV shows like *ER*. Crichton was and is considered by many to be a master of the written word, and he single-handedly shaped pop culture in the nineties. Everyone in the nineties watched the "Jurassic Park" movies and *ER*. It's undeniable that Crichton had a magic touch. A former doctor turned writer, he practically invented the technothriller genre. I consider him to be the Robert Louis Stevenson of the twentieth century. Every few hundred years, a writer comes along who captures the public's imagination with a novel that becomes part of the zeitgeist. For Robert Louis Stevenson, that novel was *Treasure Island*. For Crichton, it was *Jurassic Park*. In fact, I believe you can draw a straight line from Stevenson to Crichton. They're that similar, and Crichton said several times that Stevenson was an influence (they even both write novels that took place during the Middle Ages, for example).

In many respects, Michael Crichton is a kindred spirit for me. From what I could tell from his interviews and his nonfiction writings, we have very similar personalities and thought processes about how we approach the craft of writing and life in general.

Crichton was a man of controversy. People frequently point to sections in his work that they claim are racist, sexist, and xenophobic. I've read enough of Crichton's work to conclude that I don't think he was any of those things. If anything, he was a man of his times just like we are people of ours, and we can just agree to leave it at that.

And, we could also talk about his opinions on global warming, which I strongly believe were wrong. But we can only speculate on what he would have believed if he were alive today to see what's happening around the globe.

I believe that if Crichton were alive today, cancel culture would have come for him hard. Maybe they still will at some point. That's unfortunate. I don't care what anyone says about Michael Crichton as his legacy ages—I still admire the man. His work ethic, outlook on writing and humanity, and his contributions to the literary world were long-lasting and life-changing for a lot of readers. His contributions to Hollywood were equally so. There won't be another writer like him for a few hundred years. Writers like him are rare comets.

The older I get, the more I appreciate how nuanced people are. When I was young, I went out of my way to avoid the works of writers whose worldview contradicted my own. My mother would often watch biographies and read thick, doorstop books about historical figures' lives. I always asked her why she did it, and she told me it was to help her understand how to live her own life better. I thought that was ridiculous, and it never clicked with me until I got older and did a lot more living. Now I find myself more interested in biographies than I ever was as a young person.

As I studied Crichton, I found that I learned an immense amount from him while also disagreeing with him at the same time, often in the same sentence. That's such an interesting dynamic to have with someone. It's also a perfect mentorship.

In this chapter, I'll share some of the major lessons I learned from studying Crichton and his novels, interviews, and memoirs.

COUNTLESS CRAFT TECHNIQUES

Crichton was a master of the written word and I've learned and integrated some of his techniques into my own fiction.

Crichton taught me little things that readers never notice but that make a scene extraordinary:

- How to treat a conversation between two characters on the phone
- How to paint a three-dimensional character in less than 100 words
- Summary/abstract openings
- Pacing intensity
- How to create unlikable characters (because many of his heroes are unlikable)
- And so much more

GO PULP

．　．　．

Like many mega-bestsellers of his generation, Crichton started writing pulp novels under a pen name, John Lange. He wrote these novels while he was in medical school.

GATHER STORIES

In one of his final interviews, Crichton was asked about how he prepares his case when he wants to make a point about something (like spreading awareness about a disease). He talked about the process of "gathering stories."

For example, if I wanted to share the importance of proper strategic planning, I would start with the story of someone who didn't do it. John Smith, age 58, a data architect who wrote over 20 novels on the side and landed a hit novel that allowed him to quit his day job. When he suffers a heart attack and dies, he leaves behind a wife and three children in their 20s. Because his work was selling well, a court determines that the value of his estate is over one million dollars and his heirs have to pay taxes on it, which bankrupts them. They have to put up the family house for sale. When they declare bankruptcy, the bankruptcy court seizes John's books and sells them to the highest bidder. Now the family no longer has the rights to his books and they associate the books with pain instead of love. All because he had no idea that a court would do this. If he had, he would have made different choices.

Or, I could talk about Betty Anderson, a Generation Y writer who just graduated from college and wants to be a writer. She wants to write novels for a living but has no idea where to start. When a literary agent emails her, praising her work, she fawns and sells the copyright of her novel to a traditional publisher. Now she can't publish another book again because the book performs terribly and the publisher now owns the copyright to her book. Even worse, she can't publish another book without sending it to her agent for first right of refusal. Her dreams of making a living from her writing are severely hampered, and now she's in a depression because she listened to common wisdom.

That's how you might start gathering stories and present them if you want to open people's minds to something. It's a technique I will use in my nonfiction moving forward.

SCIENCE OVER CHARACTERS

Crichton said several times that the science in his novels always took precedence over his characters, and it's true. To paraphrase him, he said that emotional depth in writing is something that can't be done when there's a dinosaur outside your window. He believed that his characters were in a bigger, more important catastrophe, and individual traits were not as important.

It's such an interesting take on fiction that it made me think. Do I believe characters are less important in a story than the idea? I suppose it depends on the story.

It comes down to a debate between "important character" versus "important idea." Do you care more about the characters or more about something else? I don't believe there is a wrong answer.

In an interview with Charlie Rose, Crichton expressed this view, and Charlie called him out on it, saying that Crichton himself was an interesting and memorable man—he was a doctor, wrote bestselling books, made Hollywood movies, had several wives, and traveled all over the world. Charlie asked point-blank why he didn't want to make his characters as interesting as he is in real life. Crichton gave a non-answer that didn't really answer the question in my opinion.

Yet, even though Crichton says that his characters aren't as important as the science in his books, he created some unbelievably memorable characters. Dr. Alan Grant from *Jurassic Park* comes to mind. The characters in *Timeline* were also very memorable. His other novels? Maybe not so much. I still enjoyed them.

That got me thinking about how maybe there is a time and a place to have memorable characters. Maybe they don't have to be memorable in every book you write. As long as you're telling a good story and getting what you want to get across, and readers are buying it, then it doesn't matter. Many writers would see that as sacrilege, but I find it intriguing. It takes some of the pressure off your writing when you don't force yourself to create insanely memorable characters.

PEOPLE DON'T KNOW WHY THEY DO WHAT THEY DO

Crichton had a fascination with Sigmund Freud. On the one hand, he admired him. On the other hand, he didn't believe a word the man wrote. He called him the greatest fiction author of the twentieth century.

In an interview, he said something that I've believed all along: people don't know why they do what they do. He didn't know why he did the things he did in life. I wrote these exact words in my book *Mental Models for Writers* in 2017, and I was surprised to hear a mega-bestseller say them decades before me.

. . .

GET THERAPY

Crichton talks about getting therapy in his interviews. He also writes about how he sought a therapist in his memoir *Travels*. Much of his need for therapy came from his difficult relationship with his father, but he also talked about how he used a therapist as a sounding board for mundane things that somehow helped him navigate his life. At the time of this interview, Crichton was one of the richest authors in the world. If he needed therapy, then we all need it.

DON'T DIE WITHOUT AN ESTATE PLAN

Crichton died without updating his author estate plans, which created a mess for his fifth wife, who was pregnant with his child.

Estate planning will be a focus for me in 2022. Crichton taught me that.

PLOT HOLES

Crichton's work, love it or hate it, was filled with plot holes. Readers conveniently passed over many of them, but some were too obvious and headshakingly bad...even though I still enjoyed the novels very much.

Take the novel *Timeline*, about a group of graduate students who travel back to the 14th century to rescue their professor, who is trapped there because of the evil machinations of a corporate CEO. (Spoilers ahead.)

In the novel, Crichton presents time travel as space travel instead. The characters aren't going back in time; they're traveling to another universe that happens to mirror our own. Makes sense.

However, then the characters do things in that universe that affect the present day, which completely contradicts the premise of time travel to begin with.

When it was published, *Timeline* was a blockbuster hit. All Crichton fans read it. It generated an awful Hollywood movie.

Furthermore, Crichton had a traditional publisher. Did no one at the publisher say, "Wait a minute. This doesn't make sense." You're telling me that his agent, his developmental editor, copyeditor, line editor, proofreader, and oodles of other people who probably got their hands on the book didn't see this plot hole? Get outta here...

There are really only a few explanations for a plot hole this bad:

- Everyone missed it.
- Crichton had an iron will and kept it in to protect the science. He says in every interview that the science is more important than the characters, and by inference, the story.
- He/they did it on purpose to get people talking. It was a sales tactic.
- His books were so full of plot errors like this that the editors cleaned them up considerably, and what we ultimately got was a miracle.

I don't know, but if anyone tries to argue that traditionally-published books are better-produced than self-published books...

WRAPPING IT UP

Michael Crichton taught me a lot and I will forever be a fan of his work. If I'm ever half as successful as him one day, he will have taught me some important lessons that will no doubt have contributed to that success.

DICTATION COURSE

With my book *How to Dictate a Book*, I wanted to do something different.

I did competitive intelligence on all the books about dictation on the market. My biggest disadvantage is that the popular dictation books right now came out several years ago, and they were synonymous with "dictation books."

The current books went in-depth into Dragon, covered the "why" of dictation, and answered the most common questions. What else could I add to a body of work where everything has already been said?

I spent quite some time trying to figure out my "angle." What was my value proposition? Why should someone buy my book on dictation when they could buy everyone else's that have already been on the market for several years?

After some time, I figured out the angle. If I am a new writer wanting to know how to dictate a novel, is a book really the best way to learn dictation?

In other words, should I really be writing a book about this?

I decided that a book still made sense. Instead, I decided to do something that I've never done: I created a video course as a companion to the book. No email address required, no upsell other than a mention of my YouTube channel and writing books at the end of the course, and no other BS. Just click and watch. I nested the link to the companion course after the downloadable sample so people wouldn't download the sample, watch the course, and leave me hanging.

In the video course, which was approximately 10 videos with each video being up approximately less than 10 minutes each, I showed people how to dictate. I went through my dictation setup, let them see and hear several of my dictation sessions, and answered many of the common dictation concerns in video format. My rationale was that dictation has a steep learning curve, and it would do someone well to see another person practicing the art. For the cost of a cheap e-book, a writer could get all of the dictation information they needed in a 100-page book and/or a 90-minute course.

Did I leave money on the table? You betcha. But I was more curious than anything else how people would receive the book. Would they say that I was full of crap or would they find it helpful?

Detractors of the current books on the market often attacked them because the books were very short. Frankly, I think this is unfair. There just isn't that much to cover about dictation. I would be far more suspicious of a 300-page book on dictation than I would of a 90-page book on the topic. I find that beginners want more information than actually exists. Would my course help satisfy those demands?

Most creators would never create a companion course for a book and give it away for free. I've got that lane all to myself. I just charged a little more for the book than usual. I know that if I write a compelling book and offer good value for the money, it will pay dividends for me in the future because I'll have a reader who trusts, knows, and likes me. Plus, video is a natural medium for me and I know I can do well there if I can just get readers to click the link to the course.

Also, I built on the knowledge that I learned from my previous courses. It took me approximately six days to write the dictation book, and that also included filming, editing, and uploading the videos for the course. It took me almost no time at all.

We'll see what happens.

BEAST MODE RECAP

On July 1st, I began my "Beast Mode" challenge. I've decided to do it annually because it's a lot of fun.

During "Beast Mode," I write as many books as humanly possible for 90 days. I rack up big word counts and have a lot of books to show for it at the end of the challenge.

This year, I changed up the challenge:

- I introduced fiction into the mix (last year was only nonfiction).
- I let readers vote on which books they wanted me to write. Once I reached the 75 percent mark, I opened up voting for the next book.

I had some significant challenges with Beast Mode this year:
There were also some events planned during Beast Mode that I needed to prepare for:

- Two family vacations, so I had to prepare for writing on-the-go.

- Four speaking engagements during the 90-day Beast Mode period.
- A new school routine for my daughter in August, which would drastically change my household daily routine.

The first family vacation fell on the first week of Beast Mode. Yikes. We went to Orlando and West Palm, and I had to rely on writing on my phone. That worked very well, and I wrote on every day of the vacation—if you looked at my word counts alone, you would have never known I was on vacation.

The second family vacation was over Labor Day. We drove from Iowa to Wyoming. Fortunately, I didn't drive the whole way, so when I wasn't driving, I was writing on my phone.

The speaking engagements were tougher. I did have to take a week off writing to fulfill them, since they were paid engagements and I signed contracts. However, I decided to extend the challenge by two weeks to accommodate that. Problem solved.

Here is what I accomplished for this year's "Beast Mode" challenge:

- Nine books (three novels, six nonfiction books), which will be around 250,000 words
- Two additional published books that were written before the challenge
- A Writing App Database designed and developed from scratch
- A 90-minute free video course on dictation
- A 90-minute free video course on Microsoft Word macros and editing
- One article for an upcoming issue of *Writer's Digest* (which was accepted and will be appearing in Jan/Feb 2022)

- Two podcast interviews
- Four speaking engagements (*Writer's Digest*, ALLi SelfPub Con, Inkers Con, and Jessica Brody's Writing Mastery Academy)

I just love "Beast Mode."
Here are the lessons I learned:

- I applied the lessons from the 2020 challenge to this year—namely, how to write while on vacation and amid a natural disaster.
- In 2020, I wrote seven books in three months. This year, I wrote nine (which included three novels). That's 28 percent more.
- In 2020, I wrote approximately 220,000 words for the challenge. This year, I wrote over 250,000. That's 13 percent more.
- A daily minimum helped me considerably during the challenge. I implemented it halfway through. If I had maintained daily minimums throughout the entire challenge, I would have written even more.
- Much like last year, my email response time suffered during the challenge. Otherwise, my writing business worked pretty well on autopilot.
- If I kept the writing pace I maintained for the challenge, I would write over one million words.
- I also took all the books published during the challenge and compiled a limited-edition *Beast Mode Collection* and sold it directly on my website.

The big lesson I learned this year was that my writing speed is getting faster, but the quality has remained the same (editing-wise). That's powerful. It means if I keep practicing the craft and keep doing what I have been doing, interesting things can happen.

And then I thought, what if every month in 2022 was "Beast Mode"? What if I made my "Beast Mode" speed my regular speed? I am confident I can do it. What would next year look like if I did that?

Barbara Cartland is considered to be one of the most prolific authors in the English language. When she died in 2001 at the age of 99, she had published 723 books. She started publishing at 23, which is right around the same age I started (25). That means she wrote approximately 9.5 books per year. I'm doing that already—better than that most years, actually. Why not shoot to publish 724 novels before I die so I can beat her record?

I don't care what critics and snobs say. ("Anyone who writes 9.5 books per year must be a hack...") Screw them and the horses they ride on. I care about getting ideas out of my head, having fun, and building a legacy I am proud of that will provide for my family and heirs when I'm gone.

Of course, there's the issue of burnout, but I'm about as far from burnout as a writer can get. Every day, I'm having so much fun when I write, and I can't wait to sit down at the keyboard and see what's next in my stories...even when I'm not making enough money to make a living at my writing yet. Writing remains fun, and so long as it remains fun, I hope to maintain my current writing speed.

There's the issue of health and dying too, so hey, I might as well write as much as I can while I'm here.

But, back to the idea of 2022 being a "Beast Mode" Year... that's such a fascinating concept that I just might do it.

BECOME A WORLD-CLASS MARKETER

WHY TAKING TIME TO HELP PEOPLE MATTERS

My father-in-law will be ready to retire soon. In the United States, that means it's time to enroll for Medicare (senior health-care) and Social Security (senior income). Enrolling in both programs can be a nightmare to manage on your own, so many people hire advisers who take care of the hard work. This way, you can rest assured that you will be enrolled correctly and will receive your benefits.

My wife met with a Medicare adviser who helped her navigate this process for my father-in-law. She knew nothing about Medicare or Social Security, so all of this was new and challenging for her.

The adviser, an independent agent, met with her on a Saturday morning and spent an hour with her, explaining everything and how to get started. At this point, my wife hadn't committed to him and it was a pure sales call.

When she came home, she was surprised at the fact that this unknown stranger spent so much time helping her.

When it was time to buy, my father-in-law went with the adviser's services.

What does this have to do with writing? Maybe it's true that spending time with people with no expectation of a return is a helpful sales tool.

Most people are so busy that they run their schedules like despots. "I'm too busy," or "I can't spare the time to help them with that," or "I," "I," "I"...But what about *them*?

What if a reader emails you a heartfelt email?

What about a speaking event that is at a convention that has absolutely nothing to do with your genre, your career, or your ambitions?

What about that book that readers keep asking you to write?

What about giving a book away for free?

Do you have the time?

When you take time to help people with no expectation of a return, then people may choose to work with you more. That doesn't mean you should give your time away to everyone who asks, but sometimes doing things that others would never do is a smart business strategy.

TEACHING BRANDING

I spoke at this year's annual *Writer's Digest* Conference. One of my talks was about branding. It was called "The First Impression: Building a Magnetic Author Brand." The goal of the workshop was to teach authors how to think about their branding, how to build it, and how to create lasting relationships with readers.

To my surprise, it was one of the most difficult talks I've ever prepared. For starters, I was a little out of my element; I tend to do better when I am teaching writing, productivity, or apps, but I chose to do this topic because it interested me and I'm pretty good at personal branding.

I struggled to prepare material for the talk. Usually, I can find the "angle" for any talk. The "angle" is when you have an intuitive sense of what both the venue organizer and the audience want. When you nail the angle, you give a talk that crushes it on every level. The preparation is easier, the audience is more receptive, and it's more fun. When you don't nail the angle, it's painful.

I scrapped the material for the talk several times, electing for a different angle, but I don't think I ever found it.

The talk wasn't bad by any means; I delivered on my promise and I certainly think I gave people some good information. However, it wasn't my best, and that bothered me.

I discovered that branding is extraordinarily difficult to teach.

In my personal life, I excel at personal branding. I've talked about my professional career in this series many times, so I don't need to rehash it. My YouTube channel is also an exercise in personal branding. So I get it.

But it's so hard to teach because so much of branding is about your intuition.

The first lesson I taught in the talk was to figure out your story and your "why." Some people know their why, but they struggle to put together a story around it. My message was to figure out how to create a story and fail your way to the right message. That didn't resonate.

The next lesson I taught in the talk was to draw upon your work experience to build a brand. I talked about how most people know how to interview for a job (which is the ultimate exercise in personal branding), but even though the skills are the same, they can't translate that to *selling* to readers.

In a job interview, you have to:

- Explain how your experience relates to the job at hand by telling clear and powerful stories
- Write a résumé that gets past automated resume scanners and the scrutiny of Human Resources and hiring managers
- Ask for the job

To relate this to selling a book, you have to:

- Explain to readers why your book is for them by telling a clear and powerful story (in your description)
- Create packaging that gets visibility in algorithms and catches the attention of readers browsing tiny thumbnails
- Ask for the sale

The similarities are uncanny, but no one thinks about that. When writers enter the writing world, they leave their professional experience at the door, which is a shame.

This lesson *really* resonated with the audience, and I received the most questions around it.

Finally, we talked about the "common" branding stuff, like picking colors, author websites, and so on. I personally didn't like this part, and I don't think the audience did either.

When I reflect on the talk, I realized that I made a basic mistake: I was too scattered. If I ever get the chance to do this presentation again, I'll retool it.

HOW A COVER EVOLVES

I taught a masterclass for *Writer's Digest* called "The Ultimate Self-Publishing Masterclass." In it, I walked students through the process of self-publishing. I taught them how to find an editor and cover design, how to think about business, and how to market their books.

One section was on cover design, which was the most popular part. I dissected the major parts of every book cover:

- Foreground
- Background
- Title
- Subtitle/Tagline/Series Statement
- Author Name

My premise was that if you learn to think of a book cover as a series of signals, it's easier to get it right. Each of the elements I listed above gives off a reader signal. The key is learning *what* signal each one should give off, and the best way to learn that is by studying other successful self-published books in your immediate subgenre.

If you learn to isolate book cover elements, you can also provide better feedback to your designer. I shared the evolution of my book cover for my novel *Old Dark*. I shared the first draft of the cover (which was not good) and each subsequent draft until the final one, which is one of my more successful book covers. I also shared emails from which I demonstrated how to communicate with my designer.

Here is the first draft of the cover:

Here is the feedback I gave the designer:

"There's so much to love about this design, but it didn't immediately jump out as fantasy to me. At first glance it felt more like a crime/thriller cover.

I liked:

- The fact that the dragon element is the first thing that you see

- That you took an abstract approach to representing the dragon (superb) The prominence of the author name

What didn't work for me:

- The fonts Background
- Also reminded me of The Hunger Games. "

Note how I broke my feedback into short bullet points based on each element of the cover. I didn't say very much either.

Here was the next draft:

And here's what the final draft looks like:

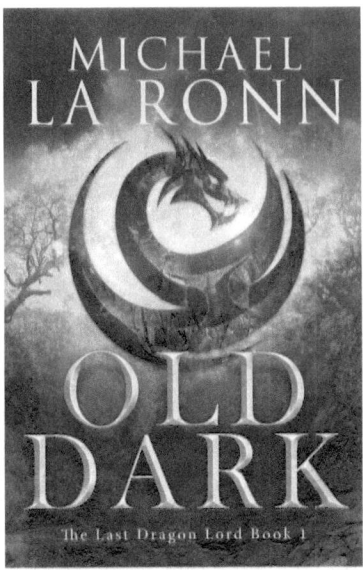

I found that the students loved to see this evolution.

I took the exercise one step further and made it interactive: I taught them how to do market research. I asked for a volunteer. I asked everyone to share a one-sentence description of their book and the subgenre. I picked one with a very clear premise and subgenre: historical fantasy based in ancient Greece. As the students watched, I went to Amazon and found several book covers that were similar to what she described. Then I took the best one and broke it into its respective elements, with feedback from the students.

Overall, the exercise was successful. It helped students think about book covers differently, and it made cover design less overwhelming for them.

The exercise was so successful that I plan to do it again.

NEVER ASSUME

The more public speaking events I do, the more I re-learn the importance of never making assumptions.

When you're speaking, never assume anything.

Never assume that your audience knows anything about your topic.

Never assume that your audience understands jargon or acronyms that are obvious to you.

Never assume that you can skip out on providing basic context.

If you do, it creates friction. When you're at an event in person, you can see friction in people's eyes and body language. Online, it's harder.

While teaching my "Ultimate Self-Publishing Masterclass" for *Writer's Digest*, my audience ranged from beginners who knew almost nothing about self-publishing to published authors. When explaining basic self-publishing concepts, I had to slow down and provide more context than usual.

I developed a rule of thumb for myself when I'm public speaking called ABC—Always Be Contexting. Sometimes all it takes to provide proper context is a few seconds. But I know when my ABC is successful because there's no friction in the room. If there is friction, it means that I need to stop and revisit my ABC because I must have said something that confused people.

Anyway, during the presentation, I found myself doing a few things that ultimately led to success:

- I never assume that people can see my screen well when I'm screen-sharing. I installed a "mouse locator" tool that puts a blue ring around my mouse, making it easier to see and follow.
- I never assume that people can see where my mouse is right away, so any time I was talking for more than a few minutes without moving my mouse, I wiggled my mouse first to help people find the blue ring.
- Whenever I wiggled my mouse, I told people I was wiggling my mouse.
- I found myself saying simple, almost childlike statements when explaining self-publishing concepts.
- I found myself reading the audience's comments and knowing what they were thinking. After a while, you learn how to read the room and adjust your speech accordingly.

The experience helped me re-learn that if you think about marketing, it's very much the same. You should never make assumptions about what your readers will do. When a reader encounters your brand for the first time, the best rule of thumb is to pretend that:

- they've never heard of you before
- they don't know what book to buy

- they don't know why they should buy one of your books
- you need to explain your value proposition to them

If you approached marketing through that lens, then you'll make different decisions about your book description, book cover, website, email communications, social media, and other marketing channels. It's a useful framework that can grow your sales.

THE POWER OF REMINDER EMAILS

I don't do a good job of promoting my Writing Power Hour livestreams. I've spoken about them in previous volumes of this series.

On a whim, I sent an email to my list letting them know about one of my livestreams. I sent the email the morning of the event, approximately 30 minutes before it started. To my surprise, I had record attendance because people saw the email and joined the link. Several people said thank you for letting them know about the event.

I did the same thing for the next livestream, and it worked again. Several people again said that they appreciated the reminder emails.

My livestreams don't make me money, and I don't get anything out of it other than a nice word count and a great time engaging with my community.

Moving forward, if I can remember to do it, I will time my monthly email communications around the power hour; that way, my audience knows that if they get an email from me, the power hour is coming up soon.

HOW I LAND SPEAKING ENGAGEMENTS

Someone wrote me recently and asked how I land so many speaking engagements. They wanted to know what I did to land them.

I had to think about it. I don't really hunt for speaking events. They usually find me.

I've only made a pitch to speak at an event once. Once, and that was for 20Books Vegas. Other than that, my strategy is to let the venue organizers come to me.

Why has that strategy worked?

First, my YouTube channel. I have over 300 videos on writing and self-publishing, and every minute of every day, someone is watching one of my YouTube videos. My entire portfolio of YouTube videos is like a sales force. They're constantly engaging, selling, and networking with people without me having to do a thing. It helps that I have decent video production, though it's not perfect. It also helped that I had two podcasts for several years; those were also excellent promotional vehicles.

Inevitably, organizers reach out to me because of videos I did years ago. As long as I keep making videos, I can keep deepening my pipeline. I like to think that every video I make is a demo of what it will be like if I speak at an event.

The second reason I attract speaking events is my speaking page. When an organizer sees one of my videos (or books) and goes to my website, I have a page called "Press" that highlights my accomplishments and recent speaking events. When possible, I include links to my prior events. I treat every speaking engagement as a calling card for the next one.

The third reason I attract speaking events is that I do my very best at every event, paid or not. I treat unpaid engagements as if they were paid, and paid engagements as if I were getting six figures. If you impress venue organizers, they'll invite you back, or spread the word about you to their friends.

That's it. I spend shockingly little time looking for speaking events. Perhaps one day the opportunities will dry up; that doesn't bother me because it just means I'll be able to spend even more time writing! Speaking is not an active part of my strategy. I love doing it and I'm good at it, but I don't want to build a career on it. I anticipate that a problem moving forward will be that I'm invited to speak to *too many* events and will have to cut back. That's why I don't hunt for events. If you look at the career of many successful influencers, they follow a predictable pattern:

- When they start, they'll speak at any venue to get exposure.
- Once they become successful, they're so in-demand, they have to start saying no to events; they're speaking frequently, traveling, and making good money.
- At some point, they burn out and stop speaking because it's too much money and effort and it takes them away from why they started speaking in the

first place: the thing they're speaking about. They walk away from a significant chunk of income and opportunities for their own mental health.

I'm somewhere between steps 1 and 2. I'm not in any hurry and would prefer not to follow the path to step 3.

THINKING UNIVERSALLY ABOUT MARKETING

I've been thinking lately about how many elements of marketing connect to form a bigger picture.

Sure, we want to sell as many books as possible, but it's quite amazing how we can integrate marketing into so many aspects of our platform.

I have been focused on the holy triumvirate lately: the book cover, book description, and first chapter of the book. Get those right and marketing becomes easier.

Here are some ways I'm trying to unlock the power of the triumvirate.

First, write a great book.

Second, commission an effective cover design using reader signals. I've discussed reader signals in previous volumes.

Third, integrate the book cover and first chapter with the book description. The first chapter is everything; the book description should reference it and the book cover should match the feel of that first chapter. Then you can also reference and match the feel with your ad copy and email marketing.

When I do market research, I only focus on the first chapter. How does the first chapter of the book compare to other similar books? What about the cover and book description? Beyond that, I trust my story to do its job.

It's easy to focus on advertising and promotion to sell books, but so much of book sales is in marketing, and so much in marketing is about little decisions around positioning and branding. My experience is that the most important marketing decisions don't cost any money other than your book cover. Thinking universally about your books can help you improve your sales.

INDIE AUTHOR = E-BOOKS AND PAPERBACKS (MINIMUM)

I was working with a family friend to help him prepare their first book for publication. He just graduated from college, and he's three years younger than I was when I discovered the joys of self-publishing.

That's encouraging. It's amazing to see young people interested in self-publishing, but there are still a lot of myths and misinformation out there.

Our first conversation went like this.

Friend: I'm going to publish a book.

Me: That's awesome! How will you be doing it? Self-publishing or finding an agent?

Friend: Self-publishing for sure.

Me: Great. How can I help?

Friend: I found an editor and cover designer, but I'm not sure how to format the book.

Me: I can help you with that.

Friend: Yeah, I really want to hold this book in my hands.

Me: [Explains how to create a paperback version of a book]

Friend: I'm almost at the finish line.

Me: Yes, you're close. Have you thought about KDP Select?

Friend: What's that?

Me: It's a program on Amazon where you can be exclusive in exchange for visibility benefits. It's a short-term tool for new authors to promote their e-book versions. From what you're describing about the book, I believe you should give it a try.

Friend: e-books? You can create e-books?

[Record Skips]

The conversation was going great, and then suddenly, we were in the Twilight Zone. He was so focused on creating a print book that he missed the biggest opportunity to make money as a self-published writer: e-books. I'm not surprised about his preference for print books (nothing wrong with that), but the fact that e-books *weren't even on his radar* was a little scary.

For the record, my friend is also a newly-minted English major. That no one even mentioned publishing e-books in an English program in one of the biggest colleges in the Midwest US should tell you something. When I graduated in 2010, no one was talking about e-books in academic circles. It sounds like very little has changed in academia in 10 years...

None of this was his fault. I coached him and brought him around to what needed to be done.

But it just goes to show you that even though *you and I* think that self-publishing is relatively common, and *we* know that e-books are essential, and that we can publish our books on great places like Amazon, Kobo, Google Play, and more, most people don't.

Self-publishing is a growing club, but it's still an exclusive club.

This chapter is a public service announcement that self-publishing properly requires an e-book *and* a trade paperback edition, minimum. I'm glad I got the opportunity to help my friend on his journey.

BECOME A TECHNOLOGY
AND DATA-DRIVEN WRITER

DEAR RETAILERS

Dear Amazon, Apple, Google Play, Kobo, Draft2Digital, Smashwords, StreetLib, PublishDrive, and every other retailer on the planet that sells e-books and paperbacks,

I have an urgent request.

I recently published a bunch of books, and the experience made me keenly aware of an issue that is present on your platform. If you fixed this issue, it would make many authors happy.

The issue? Setting prices!

When I upload a new book, I have to specify how much it costs in each currency. That's great, and I have no problems with that. However, why can't I designate a default amount for each currency?

Instead of rounding up to the next dollar per the current exchange rate, I believe it would be much more useful to designate currency defaults.

For example, if I price a book at $4.99 USD, your platform always uses current exchange rates to round to the best estimation of other currencies, like £2.68 GBP.

What if I want all of my books at $4.99 to be priced at £2.99 instead of £2.68? I can't do that. Instead, I have to type in

£2.99 every time, which, naturally, poses the danger that I might accidentally type in the wrong amount, like £299 GBP. (That's if I even remember to type in the same amount. I suspect that many authors don't price their books consistently, and that's another part of this problem.)

Please allow authors to set pricing defaults so that all they need to do is set a price in their home currency and it automatically defaults to the author's chosen price points everywhere else in the world. This would eliminate work on the author's part and make the publishing process much smoother. If an author enters the wrong price, that affects your retail sales too.

This is something that authors have needed since the advent of self-publishing, and scores of them would adore you if you implemented this feature, myself included.

If you have any questions, give me a call.

HOW I BUSTED MY WEBSITE

Readers have been asking me to update authorlevelup.com to include Secure Socket Layer (SSL) for a while now. I'm just now getting around to it. It's good to update your site with SSL because Google penalizes you in search results and your site appears "unsecure," and this is no good when people are purchasing books from you directly.

To my surprise, it didn't take long at all! It was a rather pleasant surprise. I was ready to invest several hours in the task.

All I had to do was click a few buttons on the dashboard of my hosting provider.

It was that easy...and then all hell broke loose.

Readers emailed me to let me know that links on my site weren't working. The oddest part about it was that they were links that I *knew* should have been fine because I did a sweep of my site earlier this year.

It turned out that all the links and images on my site were broken. I didn't realize that SSL affects them.

Ugh...

I had to hire a developer to help me fix the issue. I have tons of links and images on my site and I didn't have time to fix them all myself.

It took a week to fix. It sucked.

And guess what the worst part is? I still haven't updated michaellaronn.com yet!

I know what to do now, and if I could have done it all over again, I would do it differently:

- I would have hired a developer to help me with this from the beginning. They would have handled the broken links and images issue.
- The morning of the update, I would have put a banner on the top of my home page that explained I'm doing some construction on the site and to pardon my dust for a few days. I would ask people to use my contact form if they need help (and I would prioritize any emails from readers).
- After the update, I would have checked every single book page for any issues. I would have used a broken link checker plugin to help me catch any broken links. Broken links are bad news.

Anyway, that's what I would have done. The good news is that this strategy will be exactly what I do when I update michaellaronn.com with SSL!

Lesson learned.

BUILDING A CORPUS

Most forms of artificial intelligence (AI) I know of require big corpus sizes. A corpus is a body of text that is used to train the AI software. You can't train an AI with little data sets. You need very, very big ones. Like millions of words big.

That got me thinking about what it might be like for an author to have an entire corpus of their own work.

I have almost 2.5 million words published.

What if a developer could treat my entire corpus as a training ground for an AI tool they build for me? Sure, the more data the better, but I love the idea of my and only my data. No privacy issues, no copyright problems. My data is like my land—I own it and can do whatever I want with it.

I envision a tool that helps me with my editing. It reads my work, compares it to the changes an editor recommended to make recommendations tailored to my work. This is the opposite of how modern spellcheckers work—they compare your work to other users around the world, using the collective power of a network to improve its quality.

What if I could designate certain elements of style that I wanted an app to check for? Or, what if I wanted it to search only for comma issues? What if I didn't care about other people's comma usage, and I wanted to set my *own* rules?

This is possible if you could train software with your own work. We're probably a few years away from that being possible. There will be a day when developers can train AI software with smaller corpora.

But guess who has the biggest corpora of all? Traditional publishers. Since the beginning of the *Indie Author Confidential* series, I have stated that that if traditional publishers figure out AI, it will increase competition with indies.

When you think about marketing, traditional publishers own the rights to their corpus and can use it for whatever they want. They have treasure troves of data, and fortunately for them, they've digitized most of their books. They're uniquely positioned to take advantage of AI, but I haven't seen much activity yet. Probably because it's expensive, they can't see the value in it yet, and because, well, capitalism and short-term thinking.

They won't be clueless forever. When they start exploring it, it will be very clunky because they'll struggle with bureaucracy and misguided strategy at first, but eventually, they'll figure this out. It's inevitable.

But for now, I'll keep dreaming about my corpus.

EDITING DATA DEEP DIVE

This is a long and meandering chapter on editing data and there is *not* a lesson at the end. I'm just capturing my thoughts about some work I recently did on my editing analytics project.

I have my edited manuscripts for all but seven of my novels. The seven I don't have are my earliest novels. I wasn't as savvy about backing up my work then as I am now.

The previous chapter on corpora got me thinking a lot about the work I do have. I have 25 novels' worth of editing data—copyedits and proofreads. It's probably at least 5,000 edits, maybe more.

What if I could load all my manuscript edits into Excel, with each sentence in a cell? What if I could (quickly) categorize each edit by its type: spelling, grammar, format, and story?

It would be fascinating to create a chart that showed you the percentage of edits you received in each category. It would be even more fascinating to dig deep into each category. What types of words drive your spelling errors? Which punctuation marks give you the most trouble? Does your editor give feedback on certain elements of your story? How have you improved in different areas over time?

This knowledge alone would be sobering for a lot of people. Most people would say, "How can I do better than this?"

Next, I would love, love, love to overlay my edits with Word's Editor, Grammarly, ProWritingAid, PerfectIt, and my Word macro set to determine which edits each of these apps could have caught versus my editor. I didn't start using Grammarly regularly until about two years ago, and my macros are only a few months old. I believe there would be power in knowing what edits you could have caught before sending them to your editor. That's how much time you could have saved your editor.

I would also love to experiment with self-editing. I had the idea to write a novel in Word and track my self-editing changes. What percentage of the total number of edits would my self-editing account for? My hypothesis is that the number of self-edits would eclipse the number of *all* other edits by several times. I believe that the bulk of all editing happens in self-editing, which is why improving your manuscript *before* you send it to an editor is so critical.

Let's take this even further. What if, during this experiment, I could track my manuscript's progress through time by seeing how many edits each phase of editing generates?

For example (and to use simple numbers):

- Self-editing results in 1 edit per 75 words
- After Word's Editor is done, it improves to 1 edit per 77 words
- After Grammarly, it improves to 1 edit per 100
- After ProWritingAid, it improves to 1 edit per 101
- After PerfectIt, it improves to 1 edit per 102
- After copyediting, it improves to 1 edit per 200
- After proofreading, it goes from 1 edit per 225

This example goes from 75 edits per 100 to 225 edits per 100, which is a 200 percent improvement.

DEEPER INTO THE RABBIT HOLE

My next goal would be to subdivide issues down to a root cause.

Take commas. In 2018, they represented approximately 55 percent of my edits. In 2021, they were 28 percent. The reason for the difference? Grammarly—it has fantastic comma accuracy, but it's not perfect.

How can I go from 28 percent to 14 percent? What would it take to bring the number of comma-related errors below 10 percent?

When I was creating my editing workflow, I played around with the idea of a comma checker app. The *only* thing the app would check for would have been commas. I wanted to know if it was possible to program the rules or comma usage into an app.

The short answer, after speaking with several data scientists, was probably not. The best tool for this is natural language processing (NLP), which is a type of artificial intelligence. One weakness with NLP is that it isn't good at sentence clauses. While there are some workarounds, it's not easy to have software determine independent and dependent clauses. If you want to program comma usage, then you need to know the clauses. This is why I believe that apps like Grammarly still haven't mastered comma usage.

Anyway, the ideal version of a comma checker isn't possible yet, but maybe it will be in the future.

For now, it's still worth thinking about because there is a potential solution.

Let's look at my novel *Dream Born*. It's 40,000 words and it generated 245 edits from my editor. One hundred thirty-six of those edits were commas (55 percent).

There are 2,841 total commas in the book, so approximately 7.6 percent of my commas have issues. Put another way, I'm using commas correctly 93 percent of the time. Is 93 percent good? I think so, but wouldn't 97-98 percent be better?

Looking at the trends, the most common errors were with coordinating conjunctions and serial commas. I can't catch the former, but software can definitely catch the latter.

I came up with an idea: a macro that could extract every sentence with a comma to a table with the chapter, page, and line identified. I could review the sentences in rapid succession and even filter in Excel to spot problems faster.

Should I look at EVERY SINGLE COMMA in my manuscript? God, no. That would take an eternity. Like I said, I'm using commas correctly 93 percent of the time, so a sampling is best. This can easily be accomplished with a quick filter in Excel.

But what commas should I look at?

There's something else I know from analyzing my data and creating a chapter scoring model (discussed in previous volumes): I am more likely to make errors in chapters that have certain indicators (flow, important character introduced, 2500+ words, and the existence of writer's block in a chapter). What if I reviewed only THOSE chapters, and what if I did a random sampling of commas within those chapters to review (like every 10th comma).

For example, if I have 2841 commas, then I would want to look at 7 percent of them. That would be around 200 commas. Or, maybe around 100 sentences since many sentences have more than one comma.

The idea is that I might catch enough to impact the number of comma-related edits I receive.

That got me thinking about another crazy idea: what if I hired an editor *solely* for commas? It's a very silly idea, and not terribly practical by common wisdom. But what if I hired an editor to look at, say 1000 commas, which would represent the most predictively problematic chapters? How many comma-related errors would they catch?

I decided to pretend I was a comma-only editor to find out.

First, I hired a developer to write a macro that identified every sentence with a comma, extracted it to a table, and identified the chapter name, page number, and line number. I then copied that table into Excel and used a simple formula to calculate the number of commas in each sentence.

I took a random sampling of 61 sentences and read through them. In this review, four sentences needed to be corrected because there were bona fide errors. That's approximately 6 percent, and pretty consistent with my earlier stat that I used commas correctly 93 percent of the time.

I did a second sample. This time, I found 60 sentences, and five required updates. That's around 8 percent. Again, very close to the original sample and strangely consistent.

Let's talk about these results because they're impressive. I caught nine commas that needed to be corrected. If my average number of edits for a novel is 275 edits, and 28 percent of my edits on average are commas, then commas would represent approximately 77 edits. If I caught nine commas, that brings the number of comma-related edits down to 68. That's a 12 percent decrease in comma edits, and a 3 percent decrease in edits overall.

All in a trial that took me approximately 35 minutes (because you know that I love to time everything). *Nine* commas can make that much of a difference. Hot damn!

I was so stunned that I did a third trial, but with this one, I followed a hypothesis. I reasoned that the higher number of commas in a sentence, the more likely I was to make an error. More commas equal more complexity.

I took a third sample, but this time I pulled all sentences over four commas (the most was eight). There were only 30 sentences that met this criterion.

The result? Ten sentences had errors. That's 30 percent of the total!

So, in the third trial, I had fewer results, but I caught the same number of errors. That lends some credence to a rule that I should at least check sentences with greater than four commas, as they have a higher error rate. Intuitively, that makes sense. That hypothesis is probably correct.

If I wanted to make a real difference in my editing moving forward, I would:

- Do a random sampling of say, 100-150 sentences with fewer than four commas.
- Analyze ALL sentences with greater than four commas.

If such an exercise netted me approximately 19 errors (like this one did), here's where I would end up with my editor:

- 256 edits per novel (down from 275, or a 7 percent decrease)
- 58 comma-related edits (down from 77, or a 25 percent decrease)

Wow, what a difference an hour makes! When have you ever heard a writer say that something they self-edited resulted in a 25 percent decrease in edits caught by their editor? That's how you use the power of data to become a cleaner writer.

I could drive a 25 percent decrease on my own, and as I said before, I could hire a comma-only editor and push that number even higher. And I could do it at an affordable rate.

These are the types of conversations we should be having about editing in our community.

WHITEBOARDING: MY NEW TEACHING METHOD

In a previous volume, I discussed how I purchased a Wacom pen and tablet to try out a unique teaching style. This quarter, I was able to test it.

I spoke at the 2021 Annual *Writer's Digest* Conference. I did a four-hour workshop titled "The Ultimate Self-Publishing Masterclass." Students paid a fee to be there, and I covered the basics of self-publishing.

I started the session with a few PowerPoint slides, but then I switched to OpenBoard, my whiteboarding software. The whiteboard (in combination with my pen and tablet) allowed me to draw on the screen, insert images, and even do interesting things like use a magnifying glass!

Here's what I learned.

Teaching insurance classes worked wonders. In a previous volume, I discussed the lessons I learned from teaching insurance classes to professionals across the country. All the tactics I used in those classes translated to this event.

OpenBoard is phenomenal. I still can't believe this software is free. I used every inch of it, from sketching to shapes to screen-sharing to the on-screen calculator to the magnifying glass to the export feature that let me share my whiteboards with the students after the event.

The Wacom pen and tablet paid for themselves. The money I made from the event more than justified the purchase. It was a smart gamble. And, of course, I can claim them on my taxes and amortize them if I wanted.

I mimicked a technique from a comedian. I love the US comedian Sinbad. He made a courageous decision early in his career to stop cursing and make his comic routines family-friendly. In an era where comedians are expected to have dirty mouths, that's saying something. I like raunchy comedians too, but I've always respected Sinbad for that decision.

On one of his comedy specials, he did a segment where he told the married couples in the audience he would help them with marriage advice. He took questions from the audience and turned them into jokes. He did this for at least 30 minutes, in the middle of a planned routine. He had no idea what the people were going to ask, and he improvised. It was the most masterful comedic improvisation I've ever seen.

I tried something similar. During my section on cover design, I asked for all the students on the webinar to give me a description of their book. I told them I would take one of the descriptions and do market research for them live on the call so they could get some ideas what to put on their cover.

I selected one student from the list. She had a Greek historical novel. I went to Amazon and found some similar books to hers using some basic keyword searches. I then annotated the cover and taught the students how to think about covers. This exercise went over very well with the students.

People are funny about money. This isn't related to whiteboarding per se, but people criticized me when I shared editing costs because they felt my numbers weren't true to their experience, even when I caveated it. People also got mad at me for telling them about how low editor rates can go, which is baffling to me. If *you* don't want to pay a certain rate, don't criticize the messenger for sharing facts. Oh well.

If you share numbers, they criticize you; if you don't share numbers, they criticize you for not sharing numbers. Basically, you can never win.

The audience appreciated freebies. I gave them two books from my catalog and a guide that compiled all the resources I mentioned in the class. As discussed in previous volumes, I don't ask for email signups. I just give the books away. Some people do eventually join my email list, though.

The style was professional and polished. I received positive feedback from the students and the venue organizers, which is ultimately what matters.

Overall, I learned a lot from this event that I can apply to future speaking engagements.

INTERVIEW ABOUT EMERGING TECHNOLOGY

This quarter, I sat down with Matty Dalrymple on her show, "The Indy Author Podcast." We talked about emerging technology for writers. My message was that emerging technology is important and writers should be watching for watershed moments that will make technology easier to use, but that they should also maximize the horsepower of tools that already exist on their computers.

I shared how I developed my editing workflow and my sales tracking macros. I also talked about the power of thinking of books as data.

Will the message resonate? I have no idea, but it was fun to do the interview. I recommend you check out Matty's show.

AUTOMATIC RIGHTS LICENSING

When you die, who will take care of your estate? This is a huge problem that indie authors will have. It's a problem today, but it will become worse the more authors make a living from their work.

What if you provided an automated self-service rights system that lets people license rights to your work?

Here's how it would work. Before you die, you load all of your work into a database where you can designate which rights are available, and at what price.

If a magazine anthology editor, agent, or other rights buyer wants to know if your work is available, they click a button on your website that takes them to an automated portal. They can see what works are available, which rights are available, and which rights have been sold. Some works, such as short stories, might have a set price—the rights buyer selects which rights they need, enters their credit card info, and the short story is delivered to their email inbox along with the author's bio, head-shots, and other marketing materials. The email also would include legal language indicating what the buyer can and cannot do with the work. The estate would receive a separate email notification. The reasoning is that for some rights, the estate doesn't need to be involved in the affairs unless there is something complex that requires their time.

The estate might even use "make your best offer" pricing, where the buyer puts in what they're willing to pay, and if the offer is below a certain minimum, the system would reject it or make a counteroffer. All of this would happen in minutes.

To be clear, some rights cannot be sold this way—film, television, merchandise, and so on. But some could.

It's an idea that, once more authors start dying, will probably pop up in some form.

LEARNING COVER DESIGN: DETERMINING MY "TRIGGER"

Learning cover design is still on my radar. It's not a high priority, but it's not a low priority either.

I thought it would be helpful if I developed a "trigger" that would prompt me to start doing my own covers. In other words, what event has to happen for me to make this switch?

As I wrote in previous volumes, I believe we're headed for a cover designer shortage. The cost of covers and wait time goes up every few years and you don't get any more for your money. As the cost goes up, new designers charge more too. This isn't sustainable and I need to protect myself against this risk. Otherwise, it'll make the costs of book production too high.

I'll use simple, simple money to illustrate the exercise I did to help me develop my trigger.

If I were to design my own covers, it would take me at least 100 hours to learn Photoshop and cover design techniques to the point where I would feel somewhat comfortable doing it. After a few covers, I estimate that designing a cover would take me approximately five hours (and that's being conservative).

I value my time, so let's say that it's worth $50 an hour (my time is worth more than that, but I'm using simple math).

100 hours x $50 = $5000 just to learn the craft of cover design.

5 hours x $50 = $200 to do my own cover (plus design materials like fonts and stock images, so we'll move the number up to $250).

This means that it will cost me $250 to design a book cover.

What could I be doing instead of designing a cover? Well, I could be writing words. If my daily minimum is 2000 words a day, then we can quantify this even further.

Each book cover would cost me $250, 5 hours, and *at least* 2000 words of writing. If I write 10 books per year, then that's $2500 per year, 50 hours, and 20,000 words. I would lose approximately half a novel per year.

The reverse is also true: every cover I buy from a designer *saves* me $250, five hours, and *allows* me to write 2000 more words than I would have if I didn't hire the designer. Annually, hiring a designer saves me $2500, 50 hours, and allows me to write 20,000 more words.

Is that worth the cost?

The last time I checked, the average *good* cover design costs between $400 and $600 right now.

Cost-wise, using the numbers in this chapter, I'd save money, but I'd lose time and words. I'm not ready to do that yet, and, holistically, the cost of hiring a designer is still cheaper than doing it myself.

But in a few years, when average designers raise their rates again to, say $500 to $750...then I'll *have* to make the switch, designing my own covers and hiring someone only when absolutely needed. I don't like it, but I don't see any way around it.

That means I need to start learning the art of cover design in 2021 and 2022. I need to get over the learning curve so that I can be ready when the time comes. This change could be just around the corner. I hope I'm fast enough to beat it, because if I am, it will become a competitive advantage.

That said, I hope I'm wrong in predictive cover designer shortage and rate increases, but I probably won't be.

WRITING APP DATABASE

When I wrote *The Writing App Handbook*, I had an idea to create a database of writing apps that I could promote alongside the book. The concept was that users could use the database to find the perfect writing app in just a few clicks. The database would contain all the major writing apps on the market, organized by operating system, price, and features.

I sketched out what I thought the database should look like and contracted with a developer. After a short phone call, she told me she could do it and gave me a price. It was an easy job for her.

Several weeks later, The Writing App Database was born! It's a free tool that lets you search, filter, and sort by:

- Writing App Name
- Operating System
- Price and Payment Type (Flat Fee, Subscription, Free)

It also catalogs which apps have the following features:

- Dark Mode
- Splitscreen Mode
- Writing in Multiple Tabs/Windows
- E-book Formatting
- Paperback Formatting
- Autosave
- Automatic Backup
- Dark Mode
- Simultaneous Collaboration
- Outlining Support
- Distraction-Free Mode

You can also download your results to PDF and Excel, as well as in a printer-friendly format.

Of course, I also included the cover for *The Writing App Handbook* and a link to buy the book! I will also promote the database in my writing books where it makes sense.

I designed the database to be a proof of concept. If people use it and like it, I'll make updates to it. If not, it's quite good and helpful in its current form.

I have no idea how this database will be received, but it was a fun experiment that taught me a lot about WordPress and app development, which was worth the expense. This was a very cheap lesson, all things considered.

PERFECTIT AND THE CHICAGO MANUAL OF STYLE: AN AUTOMATION DREAM TEAM

Earlier this year, I tested and reviewed the proofreading app PerfectIt. I've discussed the app in previous volumes, so I won't rehash my love for it here. In short, I believe it is a secret weapon, and many editors agree with me, but most authors don't. I'll keep talking about it...

Well, this year, the PerfectIt team further validated my hunch about PerfectIt. They announced a partnership with *The Chicago Manual of Style* (CMOS). PerfectIt will check your work against the CMOS and flag errors for you. Even better, it will show you what error you potentially made, why it is an error, and it will link to the section of the CMOS so you can go and learn for yourself. Wow.

Now, I don't believe that you should follow a style guide completely. I don't agree with everything the CMOS says, and neither should you. However, consider that:

- The CMOS does pose valid points that can help make your work stronger, particularly with formatting, correct spelling of words, proper hyphenation, and so on.

- Your editor is probably adhering to the CMOS, so whether you do or not, it matters.
- The less you adhere to basic CMOS rules, the more edits you will probably receive.

Essentially, PerfectIt with CMOS integration automates the review of the manual. It pretty much ensures that you never have to read the manual to figure out what your work might need. Most authors don't read the CMOS anyway (myself included), so the fact that an app exists that helps you find additional edits is a godsend. Any edit that PerfectIt finds is one that your editor won't!

This integration is a wonderful example of automation. By simply enabling the CMOS integration, I instantly decreased the number of edits present in my work.

DRAGON, PUNCH, AND ROLL

This is a meandering chapter, but there is a point at the end.

As I was preparing for my dictation book, I did some competitive research. There are about 10 comparable books on the market that cover dictation. Some of them are quite good.

As I got deeper into the research, I struggled to figure out any new ground that hadn't been covered. I couldn't find my "angle," so to speak.

The existing books on the market are very short, high level, and focused on helping people get started. My book had to do something unique to have a fighting chance. Otherwise, people would just accuse me of writing a book to make a quick buck, and an inferior, last-one-to-the-party book at that.

I've been dictating with amazing results since 2015. How would I convey my authority and create a book that people would actually be interested in?

The critical reviews for the books said something interesting. A common theme was that the books were too short *and* full of fluff, and that they were not detailed enough. Digging a little further, it seemed that readers wanted more nitty-gritty tips, something they could not find with a simple Google search. (I don't think that's a fair representation of these books, but hey, many people said it.)

How could I find my angle, take a different approach, and create something truly unique that added to the existing body of works?

I decided to do everything all the comparable books did, but then I decided to do something that almost no one else would do.

I would write the book, which would probably be short and to the point (because there's not much to cover). But then, I would record a free, short series of videos matching the content of the book so that readers could *see* dictation in action. No email address required, no hard sell, just the usual nitty-gritty content you expect from me. I would do approximately 10-15 videos, each one around 5-7 minutes longer, maybe shorter.

Readers would be able to see me:

- explain my equipment
- set up Dragon properly
- dictate in real-time (into the dark) and show my screen so they could see what it looked like, and maybe feel better about their own sessions
- edit my work as I went
- and more

I reasoned that when reviewers said the existing books were too basic, what they were really saying was that the books did a great job explaining *why* to dictate, but they still had questions about the *how*, which can't adequately be covered in book format. By seeing how someone else does it, that might answer a lot of the *how* questions and give them some inspiration.

Anyway, that was my angle, and I felt really good about it.

I also decided to start from scratch. The dictation landscape had changed a lot since I started in 2015, and admittedly, I wasn't up-to-speed on new best practices. So I started a brand-new Dragon profile and pretended I knew nothing. I read through the 98-page Dragon instruction manual, pulled out the pieces that were relevant to writers, and then put those in the book and in video format. I stepped through the process of how I approached using the app, which ironically, was not at all how others did. That solidified my angle even more.

Then I started down another fun but weird path.

You see, I've never actually used Dragon's transcription feature. It will take recorded audio and turn it into text for you, which many people swear by.

I played around with transcription and found it to be problematic—mainly because I like to do one draft and I wasn't convinced that transcription could help me do that. If you're not looking at words, you can't correct errors.

Then I got an idea.

Sure, you can't look at words, but you can look at *waveforms*. That's what audio is. I worked with waveforms all the time when I podcasted and recorded audiobooks. Specifically, when I recorded audiobooks, I used a method called punch-and-roll to record my audio.

Punch-and-roll is a recording industry technique that studio professionals use to create better recordings in less time. Here's how it works: when you're recording audio and make a mistake, you stop recording, go back to where you screwed up, re-record (called "punching in"), and then "roll" forward from where you left off.

Professional audiobook narrators swear by this method. If they make a mistake, they stop, go back to the part of the sentence they messed up, re-record it and then resume reading.

Punch-and-roll saves an incredible amount of time because if you don't do it, you have to edit out every mistake you made.

When you're dealing with a long, long waveform, this really sucks.

Why can't writers do that with dictation? The analogy is exactly the same—everyone (and I mean everyone) who uses dictation bitches about how sloppy it can be, yet they buy in to common wisdom that it's only good for the first draft.

Why *can't* you dictate in one draft? I do all the time. And I bet I could do it with punch-and-roll.

So I tried it using Reaper, the app I use to narrate audiobooks.

I recorded a test paragraph, pretending to write a passage of nonfiction. I dictated it exactly how I would with a normal book, and I recorded my screen and voice. Whenever I made a mistake, I stopped, went back to the part of the waveform where I screwed up, and I re-recorded and resumed from there.

Then I used Dragon's transcription feature, which transcribed the text nearly perfectly with only four errors in 100 words. When I ran the text through my editing workflow, that reduced the errors to two. That's two true errors that Dragon actually made.

The entire exercise took me three minutes.

- 100/3 = 33 words per minute
- 33 words per minute x 60 minutes = 1,980 words per hour.

I did 2000 words per minute editing as I went! Of course, this number would fluctuate somewhat throughout an entire manuscript depending on what I was speaking, how inspired I was, how many proper nouns I used, and so on. But 2000 words per hour is pretty damn good. If I kept this pace, I could have done 1000 words in a quick 30-minute sprint. Yes, sir!

All because I took an audiobook technique, applied it to

fiction writing, and paired it with my editing workflow. Talk about transferable skills and using data and technology to be a better version of yourself!

And now, because I took this type of approach (in addition to hitting the basics thoroughly), no reviewer can, in good faith, say that my book is too basic or not deep enough...

BECOME THE WRITER OF
THE FUTURE

PROTECTING YOUR IDENTITY ONLINE

I read a disturbing news article about a high-ranking Catholic priest who was outed by shady methods.

Apparently, this priest had been living a gay lifestyle. He visited gay bars and used the gay dating app, Grindr.

How did anyone know this? A Catholic news organization somehow got access to Grindr location data. It's not uncommon for corporations to give their customer data to third-party vendors for some purpose—data analysis, sales, performing a service, and so on. The Catholic news organization got a package of location data and mined it to discover the priest's travels. Even though the data was anonymized, they were still able to match it to a unique ID for his phone.

I share this article not because it has anything to do with homosexuality (I don't care about anyone's sexual orientation). I share the article because it is terrifying, and it illustrates how we operate under the illusion of privacy.

If someone can do this to a Catholic priest, they can do it to you.

To relate this to writing, I think about all the apps and

services writers use daily—on their computers, in the cloud, and on their phones.

I watched an interview with John Grisham where he mentioned that he has two computers—one for his writing (that is not connected to the Internet) and one for regular consumption. He was terrified of being hacked, so he kept his work on a secure computer. Imagine if a big-name author like him were hacked. It would be devastating.

There's also the issue of revenge, or other malicious intentions. I've said for a while that it's just a matter of time before indie authors start getting hacked or hit with cyber and ransom attacks with regularity.

That article was a chilling reminder for me to review my data security practices.

THE PROBLEM WITH BEING PROLIFIC

I stumbled upon an opinion piece from 2015 about prolificacy that got me thinking.

The article is written by a literary fiction writer, who, at the time, had a debut book in the works and to date has only published that one book, aside from content in reputable literary magazines.

The article is a direct reply to an opinion piece that Stephen King wrote in the *New York Times* in support of prolific authors. I won't discuss King's opinion, but only the reply.

The article in question made the following arguments:

- Prolific authors have a big body of work and therefore more entry points, but maybe it's better that some authors' works are lost to time or unpublished rather than having to deal with the problem of reading through a prolific writer's bibliography.
- When readers like an author's work, they want to devour everything that writer has written, and

prolific writers just make it too hard for poor readers
(so therefore they shouldn't be prolific).

I'll end with a quote from the final paragraph: "It's true that telling Oates, et al., not to write so much might deprive us of great works, but the net effect is the same either way. Each new book is, for me anyway, another lost in the flood."

The article smacks of snobbery and the typical vapid attacks that critics make against prolific writers. These critics are usually people who have little to no writing experience or credentials.

The arguments in the article are idiotic at best. I won't hold the writer to the article because he may have evolved his opinions since then (or not). But I appreciate the opinion because the writer *does* (accidentally) make a valid point in the article, and that valid point is what the heart of the article should have been, but we'll get to that in a minute.

First, let's address the point of "Prolific authors have a big body of work and therefore more entry points, but maybe it's better that some authors' works are lost to time or unpublished rather than having to deal with the problem of reading through a prolific writer's bibliography..."

It's hard to put into words how arrogant and condescending this argument is. To tell a writer *not* to write, not to pursue their dreams, and not to practice their craft by publishing more books is offensive and writer malpractice in my opinion. Just because *you* don't want to wade through a bunch of books doesn't mean that other readers will care. And the least obscure books in a writer's catalog may be life-changing for someone. You have no idea how your work will impact people. Withhold your work from the world, and the universe will withhold rewarding you for it.

When you die, are people going to say "Thank you, fellow

author, for NOT publishing that book you wrote many years ago. The world is so much better for it."? No, they're going to be grateful for the work you published, and your death will probably give you a sales bump...

To the second argument of "When readers like an author's work, they want to devour everything that writer has written, and prolific writers just make it too hard for poor readers..."

It just makes me want to give writers like this a box of tissues. So *what* you have to wade through a bunch of books to find what you want to read? Have you never been to a library or browsed an online bookstore? Come on.

That brings me to the valid (and astute) point the writer made in the article, that, if he had made more forcefully, would have contributed meaningfully to the prolificacy conversation. That point is that prolific writers have published so much work that their portfolio causes analysis paralysis for their readers, and these authors aren't doing anything about it. Therefore, they're missing out on readers and readers are missing out on books they would love.

That's the heart of the issue, not whether an author should or should not be prolific. Most authors will not be as prolific as Stephen King, or, say Barbara Cartland, and that's okay. But if they choose to be, then they have a professional obligation to wield their prolificacy responsibly. That's the conversation we should be having.

Stephen King has published 63 novels at the time of this writing. Many readers have read all 63. But sure, there are readers who browsed King's portfolio, couldn't decide where to start, and bought a book by someone else instead. Stephen King doesn't need the money and probably doesn't care because he has legions of readers who serve as a recommendation engine for him, but it's a legitimate point.

A quick browse of Stephen King's website reveals no easy

way to determine which of his books to start with for new read-ers. Instead, the work is in alphabetical order, including his short stories. Very overwhelming.

(Again, if I were going to reply to Stephen King's article, and I knew he would read it, I would call him out for this. Way more productive than "No, you're wrong because prolificacy is wrong." Oh well. Missed opportunity.)

Let's take the next step up to Dean Koontz, who, at the time of this writing, has over 100 novels. Dean does attempt to solve this problem by:

- organizing his books by stand-alones and series
- offering a collector's page that contains details for completionists

He also offers a database that you can sort by title and date, which again, is probably overwhelming to a newcomer. But Dean does a much better job of trying to solve this problem.

Let's step it up even further to Barbara Cartland, one of the most prolific authors in the English language, who wrote over 700 books. Whoever manages Barbara's estate understands the problem at hand. No one (and I mean no one) is going to read an alphabetical or chronological list of her books and decide what to read. Instead, the book contains a sortable database where readers can sort books by the locations they take place in, the time period, and genre (Barbara wrote romance). The tool is stunningly easy to use. It's funny how out of all the authors I looked at, *only* the super-prolific one got it right.

Therefore, you can learn how to solve this problem NOW when you're not prolific so you can scale it.

At the beginning of my career, I knew I was going to be prolific, so I tried to think about how to make the browsing experience easy for new readers. I set out to "get the right book to the right reader at the right time." I created a tool called Book Wizard, which is a questionnaire that serves up a Book 1 in a series based on a 2-question survey. The tool worked very well, but it's time for an upgrade. I have considerably more books under my belt and I need to remain cognizant of it because every book I write increases the chance of analysis paralysis for my readers.

Here's how I can tackle that problem:

- Hyper-consistent cover design so that my portfolio has a unified look.
- Creating a filterable database like the one Barbara Cartland's estate built.
- Determining helpful ways to "tag" all my books so readers can exclude the books they don't want to read. Helping them exclude books is more important than anything.
- Including a "series reading order" when possible.
- Including a "Greatest Hits" page for easy choices as well as a dedicated experience for completionists.

Whether I have 30 novels or 300, these methods will help me scale the browsing experience. This method will also help me incorporate short stories, media interviews, and other short-form content too.

Book Wizard was a great start, but I am ready to take it to the next level when I publish my next website.

To bring this home, making the point that prolific authors need to do more for their readers is a legitimate one. This article took me 30 minutes to write, and it took me five minutes to brainstorm potential solutions to the problem of prolificacy, which is what the author of this unfortunate opinion piece should have done instead of trying to gatekeep. Trying to discourage writers from being prolific to save readers time is cynical, arrogant, and does neither writers nor readers any good.

SKINTERFACES

I read a great newsletter by The Future Today Institute about the future of smart fabrics that can interface with and influence the human body.

Got writer's block? Put on a special sweater to improve your mood.

It's an interesting technology that companies are already experimenting with. Google launched its Jacquard product and other tech companies are experimenting with this.

Privacy and security concerns aside, you can't help but be intrigued by the prospect of biotechnology for improving writing.

In Volume 2 of this series, I wrote: "The second area is writing assistance. AI has the potential to help us become better versions of ourselves. I don't need AI software that gives me generic spelling and grammar recommendations. I *do* need software that can look at all of the mistakes I've made in my past writing and help me avoid making them again. That would save me editing costs and help me create cleaner books. AI models need a lot of data, so this isn't likely possible until someone finds a way to generate better models that require less data.

Further out, imagine integration with biohacking technology. What if my writing app could track my vitals during writing sessions and tell me when it's time to stop writing because I'm too tired? Or maybe it could sense when I'm distracted and gently redirect me to another function in my writing business instead where my attention would be more productive, like marketing? If I ignored it and wrote anyway, the app could mark those sections with a recommendation for my editor to pay more attention to them and why. It would know my error rate and compare that to my vitals over time. In a sense, your writing app could assume a function similar to a nurse. Your editor would become more like a (true) book doctor, treating the most problematic areas of the manuscript. In the future, if the book has been run through developmental editing software and more sophisticated grammar and spellchecker software based on prior mistakes, an editor's approach will have to be different and more holistic."

The way the technology is evolving, I don't believe my statements were wrong.

I can already determine my past mistakes through my editing workflow. Imagine being able to hook that up to biological information. Technically, I could do that today if I wanted, using a smart watch to monitor my heartbeat, sleep, and light levels. It's not a big leap to integrate these monitors into clothing, or into data and analytics that one can use.

This is an area I'm keeping an eye on, if for nothing else than for a great entrepreneurial opportunity. ("Buy the Writer's Block Bracelet today!")

I believe it's not out of the realm that writers of the future twenty, thirty, or even fifty years from now will treat biotechnology the same way we treat Scrivener today—as an indispensable part of their workflow, and a source of data to help them manage through the mental part of writing. This is because writers face inconsistency. Some writing days are better than others and we don't always know why.

If you told someone (and proved) that you can help them optimize when and how to write by recommending the best times and days to write, based on science, they would line up to buy your product.

"Author X functions on six hours of sleep. On the days she got seven or more hours of sleep, her writing contained X percent fewer errors and X percent fewer suggestions from her editor."

"Author X is a morning person, but we discovered that they actually did their best writing at night because..."

Oh, man. That's a whole new level of technology, and it's already here in its nascent form.

ON BEACH FLAGS AND DEATH

I read a fantastic book this summer called *The Five Invitations* by Frank Ostaseski. It's about learning how to become comfortable with death so that we can live better. I heard Frank give an interview on "The Unmistakable Creative" Podcast with Srini Rao and loved it so much that I bought his book. It did not disappoint.

The main idea of Ostaseski's book is that we can become more comfortable with death in our lives if we cultivate five mindsets. Frank ran a cutting-edge hospice center for many years and helped many families and patients come to terms with death. The stories he tells in the book are gripping, heartbreaking, and inspiring.

While I was reading this book (which I bought purely out of curiosity), my grandfather passed away. I remember making a long drive to the small town in Iowa where we buried him, and I listened to the audiobook as I drove through rolling cornfields and gravel roads. It took me a while to process what Frank wrote in the book.

Shortly after that, we took a family vacation to Orlando,

Florida. We spent a day in West Palm Beach, and we visited the city Municipal Beach.

I'm not really a beach person. I've only been to a beach a handful of times in my life. When I was walking on the beach, I noticed the beach flags on the lifeguard tower. I don't know why, but I was fascinated with them. I kept staring at them so much that my wife even asked me, "What are you staring at?"

I researched beach flags and how they are used. And then I realized why I was so interested in them.

At one point, Frank talks in the book about recognizing your emotions and how they can well up inside you. The key is to understand them, acknowledge them, and reflect upon them. That helped me understand the grieving process better.

But it also helped me understand something about writing that I hadn't been able to articulate until I wrote my book *The Pocket Guide to Pantsing*.

That advice, combined with the beach flags, inspired me to write about recognizing the effects of your emotions while writing.

I'll post the passage from the book here.

Emotional undercurrents are another phenomenon while pantsing that no one told me about when I started.

In addition to story visibility, you need to keep in touch with your feelings while you're writing.

Before you write me off as a typical millennial, consider a few things.

Our feelings interfere with our writing more than we like to acknowledge. Anything that happens in your personal life will affect your writing.

However, here's what I wish someone would have told me

when I wrote my first book into the dark: feelings are like the weather. If you don't like them, just wait a little while.

Writing can be an emotional rollercoaster if you're uninitiated. Many types of feelings can manifest themselves in your writing sessions:

- happiness
- euphoria
- excitedness
- contentment
- "flow"
- self-doubt
- anger
- fear/anxiety
- exasperation
- sadness
- and more

Feelings are fleeting. You may experience self-doubt in a morning writing session, but later that night, you may slip into flow and write an amazing scene. The key is to understand yourself, acknowledge the feelings, and wait them out if necessary.

Recently, I went to West Palm Beach, Florida with my family. We spent a day at the beach. As we walked along the shore, the moody waves of the Atlantic Ocean rushed across our feet and beach flags flapped in the wind on a lifeguard tower.

Beach flags are interesting. They tell you how the ocean is feeling.

- Green flags mean safe waters.
- Yellow flags mean choppier currents and to swim with caution.

- Red flags mean unsafe conditions, such as rip-tides and tall waves.

Is the ocean always calm? No. It changes. If you don't like it, just come back tomorrow.

Your soul is a beach, and there are emotional undercurrents. There are rip-tides too—they always take you by surprise and they're pretty awful.

It's normal to experience many feelings as you write. No feeling is out of bounds. But feelings are also fleeting. They never stay for long. This is true of both good and bad feelings. Emotional undercurrents are ever-changing.

―――

It's interesting how ideas coalesce and come together. I would have never known that a book about death and a family vacation would lead me to think about writing in this way. It goes to show you that consuming media (of any kind) is always beneficial for your writing because it fills your creative well. Sometimes, things spring out of that well that you don't expect.

My readers have consistently said that the chapter in *The Pocket Guide to Pantsing* on emotional undercurrents is one of the most impactful in the book.

NOTES FROM AN "EFFECTIVE COMMUNICATION" COURSE

I took a course on executive communication and wrote down some advice that I found helpful in both my day job and in my writing life. I'm capturing my thoughts here for the future.

Think ahead in space and time. Most people can't see beyond the present (i.e., today). Others are stuck in the past. Effective executives (and authorpreneurs) must think ahead in space and time. This allows them to see things that others may miss. To do this, it's important to:

- study others in your industry
- read industry reports
- expand your perspective
- ask "what if" questions
- surround yourself with other strategic thinkers

Act decisively and courageously. Hard decisions come with uncertainty and risk, and an effective executive (and authorpreneur) must learn to be comfortable with these types of decisions. You won't always be right, but people will respect you if you act decisively and courageously.

How to act decisively and courageously:

- Make clear, justified choices
- Collect diverse inputs
- Challenge your assumptions

There were other lessons in the course that I found helpful, but these resonated the most with me.

LESSONS LEARNED IN ESTATE PLANNING

Estate planning has been on my mind a lot lately. It started when I did my taxes this year and realized I was over my head. Then I read about Michael Crichton and how he messed up his estate and excluded his pregnant wife and son because he didn't update his will. Then my grandfather passed away, and he did such an amazing job with his estate plans that it inspired me to take action.

My grandfather died with everything in place: a clear will, life insurance, medical directives, his gravestone and plot picked out, and every other detail you could think of buttoned up. In a way, he taught me how to die. He really took care of the people that he loved and he ensured that his death would not be a burden for the family. I respected the hell out of it.

If I died right now, I'd be leaving a mess. My goal is to die like he did. I don't know how long I'll live, but I can at least make sure my death is as organized as my writing life is.

Here are some lessons I've learned in estate planning.

I read *Estate Planning for Authors* by M.L. Buchman. It was a good primer on the topic that taught me good information and where to look next. The book contains a template letter that I can adapt for my heirs.

I learned that Iowa is a very good place to live and die as an author. There are two taxes my heirs will have to worry about after I die. The first is the estate tax. The federal estate tax kicks in after your estate is valued at over 5.25 million dollars. Then there's a state estate tax on top of that. Iowa does not have an estate tax. This means that I will pay no federal death tax if my estate is worth less than 5.25 million dollars.

There's also the inheritance tax, which is assessed when property is passed from one person to another. In Iowa, the tax does not apply if property is passed to a spouse or child. Also, Iowa's inheritance tax is 15 percent. Well, rather, it was 15 percent until the Iowa legislature phased it out earlier this year. I'm generally not a fan of the legislators here in Iowa, but that's a decision I can get behind!

A local law firm sums up the law: "With the passage of the new bill, if one were to pass away in 2021, the inheritance tax imposed on the inheritor would be reduced by 20 percent from the original rates. If one were to die in 2022, the inheritance tax imposed on the inheritor would be reduced by 40 percent from the original rates. If one were to die in 2023, the tax would be reduced by 60 percent from the original rates. If one were to die in 2024, the tax would be reduced by 80 percent from the original rates. And, lastly, if one were to die in 2025, the inheritance tax imposed on the inheritor would be reduced by 100 percent from the original rates, thereby eliminating the tax entirely."

This means that, assuming I live past 2025, the only estate tax I have to worry about is the federal estate tax...if my estate is worth 5.25 million at the time of my death. That's incredible.

Bankruptcy is bad. Copyrights are intellectual property, and in a bankruptcy, a court can take *any* property to pay creditors. So many authors never think of their work as intellectual property and as something that has intrinsic value, but I never made that mistake. However, this means that when I die, my copyrights will be assessed and valued by a court to determine how much tax is owed (if the federal estate tax applies). This also means that in a bankruptcy, a court will do the same thing. If you file for bankruptcy, you can LOSE your copyright. (And no, you can't transfer it to an LLC or corporation to "avoid" the court.)

What is my IP worth? Well, that's a difficult question.

I took a course with Dean Wesley Smith this quarter on Estate Planning. In it, he talks about some ways that courts evaluate intellectual property. There are many methods and there is no standardized way of doing it. You would have to pay a law firm a lot of money to determine this number, but it can be done. At least I know about it now. If I ever sign a film contract or find breathtaking success, I need to have my IP professionally valued.

Failing to plan can and will bankrupt your heirs. I read many stories of celebrities who died and, when a court valued their IP, assessed more in taxes than the estate had in cash. And then they had to file bankruptcy and lost the IP...All of this sounds silly when you only have one or two books, but the longer you do this and the more books you publish, the more real this threat becomes. Other people might laugh at me for pursuing proper estate planning, but *I'm* not going to put my family in jeopardy if I can help it. For the people who laugh at me, I feel bad for their heirs.

I re-recognized the need to be vigilant and diligent in an online world. Whenever I open accounts or purchase subscriptions, I need to be more careful and leave better documentation. I also need to track my passwords better. I do a pretty good job of this currently, but I have room for improvement.

IP management is a lucrative field. In prior volumes of the series, I talked about an intellectual property service that perpetuates the distribution and licensing of your work after you die. As I walk down the path of learning proper estate management, I'm convinced that this idea is more important than ever, and possibly the biggest need that self-published writers will have in twenty to thirty years. I'm also convinced that this is an extremely dangerous business model that can, in the wrong hands, be a tremendous force for evil. In the right hands, it could be a billion-dollar company.

Anyway, that's what I've learned about estate management so far, and I've got a lot more to learn.

LESSONS LEARNED FROM BOOKS PUBLISHED IN 2021

2021 will be my most productive year ever. In fact, I published more books this year than in other years combined.

Every book teaches me something, and I want to capture those lessons while they are fresh in my head.

Here are the lessons I learned from the books I published this year.

Indie Author Confidential Volumes 4-7. This series is easy to write and a wonderful way to bolster my word counts every year. If I do nothing else in a year, this series nets me four books per year, and around 100,000 words. In 10 years, I will have created 40 volumes. In 50 years, it will have generated 2000 volumes. If every volume is 25,000 words on average, that's 1.25 million words over my lifetime, which is completely unprecedented for a series of letters/essays by an author. This series alone could be bigger than other authors' entire discographies. The *Indie Author Confidential* series continues to be a masterclass in prolificacy for me.

Authors, Steal This Book. I repurposed the "Ideas You Can Steal" sections into a book that became a lead magnet for my nonfiction, increasing my sales.

The Self-Publishing Advice Compendium. I unpublished my book, 250+ *Writing Tips Vol. 1*, and instead, I combined Volumes 1 and 2 into a single collection, rebranded it, and made it part of my flagship Author Level Up series. I initially launched the 250+ *Writing Tips* brand as a separate series, but I decided not to continue it. Sometimes you change your mind and that's okay.

Dead Rat Walking (The Chicago Rat Shifter, Book 1). This book was a microcosm of lessons. I wrote almost all of this book while dictating on an exercise bike. It also helped me rebuild my dictation muscles. I also built my editing engine with this novel, laying the groundwork to dramatically decrease the number of errors in my work. I also experimented with fact-checkers with this book, which helped me drive higher-quality stories. Craft-wise, this novel was a testing ground for a lot of micro craft techniques, especially in the first few chapters. I adopted a thriller format for urban fantasy: first-person POV, short chapters, shifting POVs, cliffhangers. But I also kept the character-driven parts of urban fantasy. This was also the first time I wrote a brother and sister as protagonists in a story.

Rat City (The Chicago Rat Shifter, Book 2). This was one of the most challenging novels I've written to date. It was a long, intricate, fast-paced novel that kept me in the dark. I had no idea what would happen until the very end, and even the ending surprised me. Fast-paced yet extremely character-driven, it also covers weird emotional ground. It gets very dark very quickly. But it solidifies that this series is a practice ground for me. I continued to experiment with many craft techniques I've seen mega-bestsellers authors use. Near the end of the book, I switched from the third-person to first-person POV for one chapter, just to see what would happen.

Cold Hard Magic (The Good Necromancer, Book 2. I started this book in 2019, and I didn't pick it up until 2021. It taught me that no matter how long you walk away from a book, you can always return.

Spirit Chaser (*The Good Necromancer, Book* 3). This was the only book I wrote all year where there was no writer's block. I wrote it straight through with no problems. It's also the first book this year I wrote with a 2000-word per day daily minimum. I don't think that's a coincidence. I only missed one day of writing due to personal circumstances. I still finished the novel early and I never fell too far behind. I also experimented with different types of villains. This novel was definitely showier and flashier (action-wise) than the first two in the series.

The Indie Author Strategy Guide. The book was the perfect opportunity for me to revisit my own author strategy. It prompted me to draft my 2022 goals early.

The Writing App Handbook. I learned in-depth knowledge about all the major writing apps on the market, and also how to partner with a developer to create a WordPress database tool.

The Pocket Guide to Pantsing. This book taught me so much. It helped me articulate many things about pantsing and writing into the dark that I knew intrinsically but had never explained before. It was also a helpful exercise in teaching people how to do something from beginning to end.

How to Dictate a Book. This was a lesson in how to write a book in a thoroughly saturated niche. Everyone has written books on dictation, but no one wrote a book with a free accompanying course. That was fun.

The Author Editing Problem. This was the most advanced book I've ever written, with lots of numbers and data analysis, which I know most authors will not be interested in. I tried my best to warn people upfront that this book is likely not for them. I also filmed a free accompanying course teaching people how to use Microsoft Word macros.

Anyway, those were some of the many lessons my books taught me this year.

SUCCESSES AND FAILURES IN 2021

2021 was an amazing year. Compared to 2020, things "felt" as back to normal as they could be despite being in the middle of the COVID-19 pandemic.

2020 was about survival and about finding ways to stay focused on my writing. My "Beast Mode" challenge helped with that. 2020 was my best year ever productivity and sales-wise.

2021 was about building on that success, and in almost all respects, I parlayed my success in 2020 this year.

In this chapter, I'll talk about my successes and failures this year.

SUCCESSES

Productivity. I wrote a record number of books and words this year. I did this by doing what I've been doing all along—hyper-focus, commitment to learning, keeping my writing fun, writing on my phone, dictating my stories, and taking care of myself.

"Beast Mode." I wrote 10 books for my Beast Mode challenge this year.

Picking up after a long time. My book *Cold Hard Magic* was on the shelf for 18 months, and I picked it up and finished it this year. That's a success.

Streamlining. I stopped doing a lot of things this year. I stopped teaching insurance classes, podcasting, and finished law school, and ceasing these activities gave me a lot of time back in my day.

Implementing a daily minimum word count. Streamlining my life allowed me to start abiding by a daily minimum word count. It has worked wonders for my productivity. My goals are 2000 words per day Monday through Saturday and 1000 words on Sunday. I usually write well over the minimums every day.

New teaching styles. I experimented with a whiteboarding teaching style in some of my public speaking events this year, and it went very well.

Publication in *Writer's Digest*. I pitched an article to *Writer's Digest* on writer's block and it was accepted. This was my first time appearing in a print magazine. It went well enough that I got a second article accepted in *Writer's Digest*, and it will be appearing in January/February 2022.

Speaking engagements. I did a *lot* of speaking engagements this year, and except for one, they all went very well. I now have prepping for speaking engagements down to a science. Speaking at virtual events now only has a minor impact on my productivity. I did nine speaking engagements this year and still managed to write 14 books, so I'd say I've got balancing the two figured out. Some things that helped me were saying yes only to events that fit into my wheelhouse. I'm less likely to speak on odd topics now than I was in the past unless they really interest me.

Editing success. I've talked enough about reducing the number of edits my editor finds with automation enough that I won't go into it any further here.

Estate planning. My estate planning is far from perfect, but I consider it a major success that I started thinking about it this year. I took the first few steps toward cementing my legacy for decades after my death while also providing for my family, and that's something to be proud of.

New video setup. I invested in new studio camera equipment this year, which paid off in an evolution of my YouTube video style.

Eye contact on conference calls. I discovered a way to make eye contact on conference calls, which is a big deal for me since I am on conference calls a lot.

Story Bundle. I was invited to join an exclusive Story Bundle for National Novel Writing Month (NaNoWriMo) this year, which was a fun marketing opportunity, and it paid very well.

Dictation revival. I started dictating again this year, and I leveled up my dictation skills by finally using transcription. I even invented a new method to dictate cleanly and accurately ("The Pikachu Method"). This method exploded my word counts in the fourth quarter, and it should give me a nice bump in 2021.

I created my first hardcover book. It took forever, but I am now able to unlock this format, which should help increase my sales over the long term.

Permafree. I experimented with a permafree nonfiction book that improved my sales.

Backing up my work. I invested in new hardware to back up my work this year.

FAILURES

Video consistency. My YouTube channel was one of my casualties this year. While I haven't stopped making videos, I have stopped making *edited* videos right now. Finishing law school and starting a new job threw off my publication schedule.

Video content quality. While my video quality has improved, my YouTube content quality has not. It's a missed opportunity for me to get back up-to-speed with YouTube best practices.

Taxes. I had a win with my taxes and a major loss. I didn't hire the right accountant and I had to redo their work. I covered this in previous volumes of the series. I ended up okay, but it was a sobering lesson learned.

Email management. I completely lost control of my email inbox this year. I still haven't figured out a way to solve the problem.

One public speaking engagement didn't go well. I think it was just a bad audience fit. My message didn't land at all, and the participants were downright hostile. I probably should have seen it coming, but you live and you learn.

Email newsletters. I didn't send out regular newsletters this year to my audience, and that was a missed opportunity for sales.

Too many priorities. My 2021 strategy had five pillars. It was too much to keep track of. I'll discuss this further in my 2022 strategic priorities.

Unorganized. I'm more organized than most, but I still have significant opportunities. I need to reorganize all my files, clean up my platform, and make some updates to improve my author professionalism. There's always room to be better.

Losing weight. I lost a few pounds this year, but I have a long way to go. I suppose this could also be viewed as a success!

Those are my successes and failures for 2021. Here's to a good 2022.

Q4 PROGRESS REPORT

It's time to provide an update on the progress I've made toward my goals in 2021.

I accomplished a lot this year, but I did not hit all of my goals. That's mainly because I set so many of them. I very much viewed this year as a transition year into a smoother strategy. I also did some course-correcting mid-year. Next year, I will set fewer goals and hopefully will achieve all of them.

MY STRATEGY

My mission is to educate and entertain my audience in the genres I write, and to remain nimble in an ever-changing industry.

I will achieve my mission through five strategic priorities:

- Become a world-class content creator
- Become a world-class marketer
- Become a technology-driven writer

- Become a data-driven writer
- Become the writer of the future

WORLD-CLASS CONTENT CREATOR

Goal: 64 books published by 12/31/2021. I'm currently at 65 books for the year with the potential to write at least one or two more before the year ends, so I exceeded my production goal.

Develop a way to ensure consistency across my platform. I started this in Q4, but I won't finish it this year. I course-corrected mid-year because I realized that I need to do a lot of cleanup on my platform before I start standardizing things. For example, I need to refresh some covers, book descriptions, website pages, and so on. This will be a key priority for me in 2022.

WORLD-CLASS MARKETER

Grow my Amazon Ad imprint. Completed.

Improve my copywriting skills. Completed.

Reduce my tax liability. Successfully failed (and completed). See Volume 5 for more information.

BECOME A TECHNOLOGY-DRIVEN WRITER

. . .

Develop an automated way to enforce consistency. Completed.

Redesign my Book Wizard tool on Michael La Ronn.com and Author Level Up.com. Not started, but I'm glad I waited because the Barbara Cartland Database gave me some great ideas on how to manage my books on my website. I think I can do it for cheaper than I originally estimated.

Implement a flexible book database that houses all the metadata for my books. I started this work but did not finish it. This ties in to the cleanup I need to do on my platform and this work will be rolled into that.

Automate my bookkeeping. Successfully completed.

BECOME A DATA-DRIVEN WRITER

Make minor enhancements to my sales database. Completed.

Invest in learning the basics of Python, Webhooks, and Application Programming Interfaces (APIs). Completed.

BECOME THE WRITER OF THE FUTURE

Read 50 books. Completed.

Implement direct print and audiobook sales on my website. Did not accomplish.

Complete my law degree. Completed.

Complete 12 WMG workshops to improve my writing craft. Completed.

BRINGING IT ALL TOGETHER

All told, I did a great job sticking to and executing on my goals this year, and my author business is better for it.

On the way to becoming a world-class content creator, I produced a copious number of books that will forever be a part of my legacy. I now have 65 books published to my name and over 2.5 million words published. I also experimented with multimedia content to help readers enjoy my books better. I also experimented with new teaching methods that will make my public speaking better.

I've laid the groundwork for a way to standardize all of my content so that everything is consistent and I can keep better track of it. Prolificacy breeds all sorts of problems, but I'm well-positioned to deal with it better than most.

On my way to becoming a world-class marketer, I made a killing with Amazon Ads and cut my copywriting time in half with my Sales Builder tool. I also reduced my tax burden, ensuring that I keep more money in my bank account.

On my way to becoming a technology-driven writer, I explored ways to "get the right book to the right reader at the right time" (that I discussed in this book). I'm on my way to developing a database that houses all the important metadata for my books that will become both a database and the engine for creating the 2.0 version of my websites so that I no longer have to "create" book pages myself. Book page management is the biggest time suck in maintaining an author website, and this year, I think I came up with an idea to solve that. I also automated my bookkeeping by creating a process that automatically archives and tags all my expenses.

On my way to becoming a data-driven writer, I learned the basics of the Python programming language and application programming interfaces (APIs). These will be critical skills in the coming age of AI.

On my journey to becoming the writer of the future, I read over 50 books of fiction and nonfiction, instilling in me endless interesting ideas that will emerge creatively someday in the future. I also learned a lot about many different random topics, which will help me become a better writer because they expanded my awareness of the world.

I completed my law degree, which made me a more business-savvy writer.

I completed 12 workshops by Dean Wesley Smith and Kristine Kathryn Rusch at WMG Publishing, and their craft workshops have immeasurably improved my craft.

I completed a "virtual" mentorship with Michael Crichton, a mentor who taught me some important craft and business lessons that I am now using in my writing business and will carry with me.

I also streamlined my responsibilities, giving up teaching insurance classes and podcasting so I could devote more time to writing books. As you can see from my productivity this year, both of those things resulted in a banner year. I saw results approximately six months after ceasing those activities.

If you'd like to see the goals I set for 2021 on a mind map, visit

www.authorlevelup.com/2021strategy

In the next chapter, I'll cover my 2022 strategy.

MY 2022 STRATEGIC PRIORITIES

If 2020 was about survival and staying focused and 2021 was about building on success, 2022 is about creating stability and a new normal.

In 2022, I'll reap the full benefits of being done with law school, podcasting, and insurance classes. I'll have a lot more time to focus and streamline my operations so that I'm moving faster in the direction I want to go.

As such, I evaluated my goals for 2021 and need to make some changes.

First, five pillars is too many. They worked very well for me in 2020 because they helped me stay focused, but I don't need five strategic priorities anymore. I'm reducing my focus down to two. This is a radical shift, but it's needed.

Moving forward, my strategy will be as outlined in this chapter.

My mission is to educate and entertain my audience in the genres I write, and to be the author that readers think of when they're looking for a new book to read.

I will achieve my mission through two strategic priorities:

- To become a world-class content creator
- To become a technology and data-driven writer

WORLD-CLASS CONTENT CREATOR

To achieve my goal of becoming a world-class content creator, I will focus on the following tactical priorities:

- Demonstrate a commitment to learning the craft of storytelling and teaching
- Demonstrate a commitment to outstanding quality AND quantity
- Examples of day-to-day activities that will help me carry out my tactical priorities include:
- Keep learning through online courses and workshops taught by professional writers who are further down the path I want to write
- Reading
- Developing mentorships
- Finding new ways to increase my daily word counts
- Mastering different writing methods
- Documenting my process of becoming a successful writer in the *Indie Author Confidential* series
- Cleaning up my platform to ensure a consistent quality reader experience

BECOME A TECHNOLOGY AND DATA-DRIVEN WRITER

To achieve my goal of becoming a technology and data-driven writer, I will focus on the following tactical priorities:

- Use technology to make the business more efficient
- Use data to get insights

Examples of day-to-day activities that will help me carry out my tactical priorities include:

- Developing a tax plan
- Developing an estate plan assisted with technology
- Learning how to design my own covers
- Hiring a personal assistant for small tasks where it makes sense
- Developing a metadata database for my work
- Improving my readers' experience on my website
- Implementing direct sales for my fiction

You'll notice that "become the writer of the future" is not an explicit category. It's still a priority, but here's how I see it: if I become a world-class content creator and a technology and data-driven writer, I'll *become* the writer of the future.

As I move into 2022, I'll adjust the structure of *Indie Author Confidential*:

- World-Class Content Creator
- Technology and Data-Driven Writer
- Looking Forward

The "Looking Forward" section will function much like "Become the Writer of the Future," with me opining on miscellaneous items that don't fit into the other two categories but that I'm paying attention to.

Future volumes of *Indie Author Confidential* may be a little shorter, but that serves my goals.

I'm excited for 2022. You never know what a new year will bring, but I've put my author business in a great position and I'll be able to start the year strong.

CONTENT CREATED WHILE WRITING THIS BOOK

Books

The Writing App Handbook

M.L. Ronn covers the most important features of writing apps on the market, and what to look for when you are shopping for a writing app. It also comes with a free writing app database you can use to help you find the perfect match.

Buy at www.authorlevelup.com/handbook.

Access The Writing App Database at www.authorlevelup.com/writingapps.

The Self-Publishing Advice Compendium

(This book contains 250+ Self-Publishing Tips Volumes 1 and 2, but has been rebranded). In this self-publishing advice guide, M.L. Ronn covers 500+ writing, publishing, and marketing tips to help you perform at your very best.

Buy at www.authorlevelup.com/compendium.

. . .

The Indie Author Strategy Guide

Learn how to craft a winning strategy for your author business by developing a mission and vision statement, sound strategic priorities, and key tactics.

Buy at www.authorlevelup.com/strategy.

The Pocket Guide to Pantsing

Discover how to write a novel without an outline and feel amazing doing it. Building on the concepts that Dean Wesley Smith teaches in his groundbreaking book *Writing into the Dark*, M.L. goes deep, deep, deep into the rabbit hole to give you strategies and tactics on how to write a great novel without an outline every time.

Buy at www.authorlevelup.com/pantsing.

How to Dictate a Book

M.L. Ronn covers his process of dictation and breaks it down in this short and easy-to-understand volume. It also comes with a complimentary 90-minute video course to help you see dictation in action.

Buy at www.authorlevelup.com/dictationbook.

Podcast/Video Appearances

"Bringing a Creative Endeavor to an End" with Michael La Ronn. The Indy Author Podcast with Matty Dalrymple.

In this interview, Michael discusses how and why he decided to end his two podcasts, "The Writer's Journey" and "Writing Tip of the Day."

"Emerging Tech for the Indie Writer" with Michael La Ronn. The Indy Author Podcast with Matty Dalrymple.

In this interview, Michael discusses emerging technology he's watching for his writing business.

"Questions for Black Authortubers." Zarina Macha's YouTube channel.

In this montage interview, Michael talks about his experience being a black authortuber, and what it's like to write books and make YouTube videos as a black creative.

"How to Write Nonfiction." Self-Publishing Advice Conference October 2021.

In this interview, Michael turns the tables and interviews fellow nonfiction writer and friend Dale L. Roberts about how to write nonfiction and how to craft a compelling message. (This video is behind a free registration and I do not know how long it will be available).

READ THE NEXT VOLUME

Michael's writer journey continues in the next volume of this series!

Grab your copy at www.authorlevelup.com/confidential.

MEET M.L. RONN

Science fiction and fantasy on the wild side!

M.L. Ronn (Michael La Ronn) is the author of many science fiction and fantasy novels including *The Good Necromancer, Android X,* and *The Last Dragon Lord* series.

In 2012, a life-threatening illness made him realize that storytelling was his #1 passion. He's devoted his life to writing ever since, making up whatever story makes him fall out of his chair laughing the hardest. Every day.

Learn more about Michael
www.authorlevelup.com (for writers)
www.michaellaronn.com (fiction)

MORE BOOKS BY M.L. RONN

Books for Writers:

www.authorlevelup.com/books

Fiction:
www.michaellaronn.com/books

YOU MIGHT ALSO ENJOY BE A WRITING MACHINE

The no-nonsense, no BS guide to becoming a prolific author--available in ebook, paperback, and audiobook!

Do you want to write a lot of novels, but can't improve your writing speed?

Writing fast is the most important skill you can develop as a writer. While it seems hard to hit high word counts, the secrets are easier than you think.

In this writer's guide, prolific author M.L. Ronn pulls back the curtain on the process that he uses to write 6-8 novels a year. He has kept this pace while juggling responsibilities as a husband, father, manager at a Fortune 100 company, and a law school student. The result is a catalogue of over 40 books and counting.

- Create a writing habit that suits your lifestyle
- Use writing apps on your phone to double your word count
- Learn strategies to beat writer's block forever
- Discover how to write smarter by using unorthodox strategies used by the masters

This book is the only thing standing between you and your writing dreams. Write faster, write smarter, beat writer's block, and be the prolific author you've always wanted to be!

Grab your copy of *Be a Writing Machine* today. Available in ebook, paperback, and audiobook formats at your favorite retailer: www.authorlevelup.com/beawritingmachine

www.ingramcontent.com/pod-product-compliance
Lightning Source LLC
Chambersburg PA
CBHW020253130626
46549CB00005B/2201